PANDORA, PENELOPE, POLITY
HOW TO CHANGE THE EUROPEAN UNION

About the author

Andrew Duff was a British Liberal Member of the European Parliament from 1999-2014. He served in the Convention on the Charter of Fundamental Rights and in the Convention on the Future of Europe. He was one of Parliament's representatives at the Lisbon Intergovernmental Conference. From 2008-13 he was President of the Union of European Federalists. Before becoming an MEP he was Director of the Federal Trust. He is a member of the European Council on Foreign Relations.

Among his publications are: *Maastricht and Beyond: Building the European Union* (with John Pinder & Roy Pryce), 1994; *The Treaty of Amsterdam*, 1997; *Reforming the European Union*, 1997; *The Struggle for Europe's Constitution*, 2005; *Plan B: How to Rescue the European Constitution*, 2006; *Saving the European Union: The Logic of the Lisbon Treaty*, 2009; *Post-national democracy and the reform of the European Parliament*, 2011; *On Governing Europe*, 2012.

He led the Spinelli Group team which wrote *A Fundamental Law of the European Union* in 2013.

PANDORA, PENELOPE, POLITY

HOW TO CHANGE THE EUROPEAN UNION

Andrew Duff

JOHN HARPER
PUBLISHING

Published by John Harper Publishing
27 Palace Gates Road
London N22 7BW, United Kingdom.

www.johnharperpublishing.co.uk

Distributed by Turpin Distribution Services Ltd.

Pandora, Penelope, Polity: How to Change the European Union

ISBN 978-0-9929748-6-2

Typeset in 9pt/11pt. Palatino

Printed and bound in the EU at the Gutenberg Press, Malta.

TABLE OF CONTENTS

PREFACE

This book was made possible by my being dispossessed of a seat in the European Parliament at the May 2014 elections. My enforced moment of reflection has coincided with the change of guard in the EU institutions from Barroso to Juncker and from Van Rompuy to Tusk and from Schulz to, well, Schulz. At home, Scotland has voted to stay in the United Kingdom, at least for now. The British general election, which will shape the decision about whether the UK stays a member of the European Union, is still a few months ahead. The euro crisis which has dominated our lives for the last number of years rolls on, changed but unresolved. As does the problem of Russia.

The aim of the book is to encourage a serious debate about the future of our new European polity. It advocates a federal union, and warns against other less ambitious choices. It draws on our rich, recent experience of reforming the Union through constitutional ways and means – some more successful than others. It makes an initial assessment of the Treaty of Lisbon in practice, and suggests a mandate for a new Convention which will have to do the heavy lifting at the next round of treaty change.

The book has been fashioned by my very many discussions with colleagues in the European Parliament, the Commission and Council, with a rich array of Brussels think-tanks and journalists, and with my former assistants and students. Thanks are due to Peter Ludlow for involving me in the European Strategy Forum and to Janis Emmanouilidis for the same in the New Pact for Europe project. I am particularly grateful to those with whom I collaborated to produce the 'Fundamental Law' of the Spinelli Group in September 2013. Special mention is due to Paolo Ponzano who organised a symposium at the Robert Schuman Centre at the European University Institute in Florence in November 2013, and to Thomas Fischer of the Bertelsmann

Stiftung who organised a round table of Brussels thinkers and doers in January 2014. Pieter Van Nuffel told me things about Penelope I did not know. John Harper jumped at the chance to publish about her and Pandora. Sietse Wijnsma read the text, but the mistakes are still mine.

Readers are welcome to send comments on the book to andrewduff@andrewduff.eu or to @AndrewDuffEU.

Andrew Duff

November 2014
Cambridge and Brussels

INTRODUCTION

2014 has been a year of institutional renewal in the European Union. Now that the new leadership is in place, it is time to look again at its long-term political prospects. This is not an academic exercise but a democratic necessity. The EU suffers from structural flaws, not least concerning the current arrangements for economic and monetary union, which the financial crisis has put under strain. It is clear that the Treaty of Lisbon, in force for just five years, has not solved all the problems of EU governance, and the new treaty is already in some important respects being stretched to its legal limits. Europe still lacks a sound constitutional framework for the establishment of fiscal and eventually political union.

The Union's previous approach to deeper integration has been largely incremental – creeping change when forced to do so. According to Antonio Vitorino, the distinguished constitutional lawyer, such incrementalism admits of 'as much federalism as needed, but as little as possible'. In this constitutional story the position of Germany has been crucial. Without exception German chancellors have been adept at finding European solutions to common problems. Angela Merkel, the current chancellor, is also very good at buying time, but as one of her senior advisors concedes, the danger is that 'we are now buying time but not using it'. In the meantime, Europe slips down the global competitiveness league; its population is fast ageing; and the EU's early promise of leadership in international affairs has not been fulfilled. The euro crisis mutates – yet it persists. The popularity of the Union wanes, even to the point that one of its largest member states is thinking of leaving.

It is the contention of this book that treaty change is necessary and cannot be long avoided if a more united Europe is to be well governed. We will try to spell out why treaty change is needed, what it may comprise and how it might be done.

A general revision of the treaties is complex and (constitutional lawyers aside) may be unpopular. It can scarcely be attempted if there is not a very good chance of success. We trace the recent history of amending the EU treaties, and examine some of the better proposals for reform. We argue that European integration has now reached the point where the EU needs a proper government if it is to survive and prosper for the sake of its states and citizens over the long term. That government must be federal if the EU is to be really democratic.

The idea of federal government is strangely controversial. While federalism is adopted as the preferred form of government in many liberal democratic countries across the globe, the European élite is nervous about embracing the federal idea for their own European Union. Indeed, contemporary political thought in Europe, such as it is, seems to have discarded federalism as a subject worthy of debate. No national political party now campaigns for European federalism; even Europe's academics seem to have all but abandoned the discipline of federal studies. With few exceptions, serious analysis of European integration is now confined to lawyers and economists; political philosophers have largely given way to pundits and pollsters.[1]

Patti chiari, amicizia lunga

So to define terms (lest others do so) by 'federal' we mean that constituent states pool elements of national sovereignty centrally over a range of competences which, contemporary circumstances prevailing, are more usefully governed in common than separately. As circumstances change, so federal competences may fluctuate, but the power of the central government – in this case, the EU institutions – must be capable of taking and executing effective decisions in the general interest of the whole union. Before taking action, the federal authority must apply the test of subsidiarity concerning added value and efficacy. In a federal union, federal law has primacy in those areas of conferred competences. But the federal power respects the autonomy of

---

1   Honourable exceptions would include Jürgen Habermas, George Soros and J.H.H. Weiler.

the member states to act within the bounds of their competence, and while the central government may dominate in agreed areas, it shall never be hegemonic. Federal government is coordinate with and not imposed upon the system of multi-level governance. Federal citizenship is equal and plural. Minorities are privileged in a federation lest they be subsumed by it. Democratic and judicial checks and balances are strong and are written down in a good constitutional treaty: clear pacts mean long friendships.

Federalism is not a panacea. There are inevitably tensions between the different federal entities, which only successful unions can manage well. Although the European Union contains many federal elements, federalism has not since the early years been endorsed systematically or with conviction by its member states who seem content to remain, in confederate mode, 'masters of the treaties'. Accordingly, the EU still has many characteristics of a classical inter-state alliance, run by ill-coordinated national governments, in which inevitably the larger and richer states predominate.

This book seeks to explain why a federal union is today the best, if not the only form of governance for a large, strong and successful European Union. It argues that the EU needs urgently to prioritise its search for a government, and that that government is best centred on the federal model of the European Commission and not on the confederal model of the European Council.

We are critical of those who would rather muddle on through current difficulties without radical reform because they are afraid of opening Pandora's famous Box. Pandora, if you remember, was the first woman to be created by Zeus. Understandably curious when given a gift box by the gods, the lady opened it – only to let out all the evils of the world. Only Hope was left. It is strange that, so many years later, urbane modern leaders of Europe are still gripped by a fear of being unable to control events of their own making.

Penelope, our other lady, was the wife Odysseus abandoned when he went off to fight the Trojans. During the twenty-year wait before her husband returned (somewhat unexpectedly), Penelope tricked her many suitors into accepting her refusal of their advances by claiming she had to finish knitting a shawl. Every night the stoic and faithful lady unstitched what she had stitched by day. Penelope's endless travail was to no obvious purpose – but in the end they all lived happily ever after. Penelope has another purpose in this book, along with somewhat less mythical characters like Altiero Spinelli.

1. MISSING A CONSTITUTIONAL MOMENT

The Treaty of Lisbon eased into force, eleven months late, on 1 December 2009. The event was celebrated with speeches and fireworks on the Tagus waterfront at the Tower of Belem. It was the culmination of a long and fairly exasperating period of reflection, negotiation, conciliation and compromise which had started at the Laeken European Council in December 2001, proceeding with the Convention on the Future of Europe in 2002-03, before moving to an agreement on a Treaty establishing a Constitution for Europe – the Constitutional Treaty, as it was generally known – in 2004 which was then stymied, in 2005, by referenda in France and Holland. After much kerfuffle, the Lisbon treaty was signed on 13 December 2007, but its ratification was delayed by an Irish No in a referendum in June 2008. Fifteen months later, and after having received assurances in the form of a Protocol that the treaty in fact meant what it said, the Irish had another go and judiciously changed their mind.[2] In Germany, the treaty had to pass the hurdle of its Federal Constitutional Court.[3] The Czech Republic was the last to ratify in November 2009 once President Vaclav Klaus overcame his own rearguard action against the treaty – but not before he

2   The Protocol on Ireland's 'guarantees' was glued on to the end of the Lisbon treaty at the same time as the Croatian accession treaty was signed in December 2011.

3   Judgment on 30 June 2009, Bundesverfassungsgericht, BVerfG, 2 BvE 2/08. http://www.bverfg.de/entscheidungen/es20090630_2bve000208en.html

had extracted from the European Council a decision to add his country as a signatory to a controversial British Protocol which seeks to dilute the force of the Charter of Fundamental Rights.

This chapter tells the story of how that original Constitutional Treaty came to be written. Although the Constitutional Treaty was never ratified, much of it survived to be transplanted into Lisbon – a testament to the quality of the original.

The European Union had only recently stumbled through three difficult Intergovernmental Conferences (IGCs) – at Maastricht in 1991-92, Amsterdam in 1996-97 and Nice in 2000. Each successive reform of the treaties was worse than the one before.[4] The scope of the package slimmed and the quality of the deal deteriorated. Each treaty negotiation concluded with a commitment to doing better next time – a habit which bore witness to the strength of the perennial goals of integration as well as to the frustrations experienced in reaching them. Amsterdam had been conceived by the Treaty of Maastricht, which provided for a new IGC to be convened in 1996.[5] A Protocol to the Treaty of Amsterdam laid down that before the membership of the European Union exceeded twenty, another Intergovernmental Conference should be convened 'to carry out a comprehensive review of the provisions of the Treaties on the composition and functioning of the institutions'.[6] To reinforce the point, the governments of Belgium, France and Italy had appended a Declaration to the Treaty of Amsterdam asserting that the treaty 'does not meet the need … for substantial progress towards reinforcing the institutions'.[7]

At Nice, at the end of a particularly long and fractious IGC, a Declaration was agreed that committed the leaders to conduct a 'deeper and wider debate about the future of the European Union' and to make a more considered declaration in one year's time on the 'continuation of this process'.[8] Four items were picked out for special treatment: a more precise delimitation of powers between the EU and its member states, reflecting the principle of subsidiarity; the status of the Charter of Fundamental Rights; a simplification of the treaties with a view to making them clearer and better understood without changing their meaning; and the role of national parliaments 'in the European archi-

---

4   For a chronology of EU treaties see Annex One.
5   Article N.2 (later Article 48) of the Treaty on European Union.
6   Article 2, Protocol on the institutions with the prospect of enlargement.
7   Declaration No. 57 of the Treaty of Amsterdam.
8   Declaration No. 23 of the Treaty of Nice.

tecture'. The Declaration suggested that a new IGC would be convened in 2004, but frustration with the IGC process was voiced more widely, not least in the European Parliament, which had called for the establishment of a proper constitutional convention even before the debacle of Nice.[9] So the European Council, meeting in Gothenburg in June 2001, agreed to broaden participation in the preparation of the next IGC and even to consider the creation of what it called an 'open forum'. The Swedish presidency included as one option for this open forum the Parliament's idea of a Convention, modelled on the one that had drawn up a Charter on Fundamental Rights in 1999-2000.

The Laeken Declaration

On 14-15 December 2001 Europe's national leaders met in Laeken to consider all these questions afresh. Present were the heads of state or government of the fifteen member states of the European Union, the twelve 'accession states', and the 'candidate' state of Turkey. The European Council, chaired by Guy Verhofstadt, issued an eight-page 'Laeken Declaration on the Future of the European Union'. This had been drawn up by the Belgians with the advice of a group of 'wise men'.[10] Although somewhat wordy, the Declaration eventually reaches its destination: a decision to set up a special Convention 'composed of the main parties involved in the debate on the future of the Union' whose task was to 'consider the key issues arising for the Union's future development and try to identify the various possible responses'.

The Laeken Declaration identified three basic challenges: 'how to bring citizens, and primarily the young, closer to the European design and the European institutions, how to organise politics and the European political area in an enlarged Union and how to develop the Union into a stabilising factor and a model in the new, multipolar world'. Specifically, the Declaration wanted the Convention to 'clarify, simplify and adjust' the division of competences between the Union and its states. 'This can lead both to restoring tasks to the Member States and to assigning new missions to the Union, or to the extension of existing powers, while constantly bearing in mind the equality of the Member States and their mutual solidarity.' It wondered how na-

9   European Parliament Resolution (Duhamel Report) on Constitutionalisation of the Treaties, 25 October 2000, A5-0289/2000.
10   Giuliano Amato, Jean-Luc Dehaene, Jacques Delors, Bronislaw Geremek and David Miliband.

tional spheres of competence could be protected against 'creeping expansion' of EU competence. No specific suggestions were made of policies that could be repatriated to member states, although the question was posed as to whether the 'day-to-day administration and implementation of the Union's policy [should] be left more emphatically to the Member States'.

The Declaration went on to propose the need for a sharper distinction between executive and legislative measures, including a return to the framework nature of the EU directive whereby the EU established common aims but member states find the ways and means to achieve them. The idea of the looser open method of co-ordination – introduced by the Amsterdam treaty at a time of more than usual weakness of the Commission – was commended. Turning to the institutions, Laeken asked a great many pertinent questions without providing answers. These involved the executive authority and democratic legitimacy of the European Commission, the extent of the co-decision procedure between Council and Parliament, electoral reform of the Parliament, transparency in the Council, the presidency of the Council and the role of national parliaments.

As a mandate to the Convention, the Laeken Declaration was problematic. On the one hand, the Convention was invited to simplify the treaties without changing their meaning; on the other hand, it was asked to consider amendments to the various policies. The European Council wanted the Convention to give easy constitutional answers to some difficult political questions. One issue was the possibility of making a distinction between a basic treaty and other treaty provisions, possibly with different amendment and ratification procedures. Another concerned the status of the Charter of Fundamental Rights drafted by the first Convention but which had been accepted by the IGC at Nice, only one year previously, as a mere code of conduct without mandatory effect. Lastly, the heads of government steeled themselves: 'The question ultimately arises as to whether this simplification and reorganisation might not lead in the long run to the adoption of a constitutional text in the Union. What might the basic features of such a constitution be?'

Hedging its bets, the European Council concluded: 'The Convention will consider the various issues. It will draw up a final document which may comprise either different options, indicating the degree of support which they received, or recommendations if consensus is achieved. Together with the outcome of national debates on the future of the Union, the final document will provide a starting point for discussions in the Intergovernmental Conference, which will take the ultimate decisions'.

The Convention on the Future of Europe

Before leaving Laeken, the European Council appointed Valéry Giscard d'Estaing as president of the Convention, and Giuliano Amato and Jean-Luc Dehaene as vice-presidents. John Kerr, a British official, was appointed secretary-general. The rest of the Convention was composed of representatives of the heads of government, two national parliamentarians from each state, sixteen representatives of the European Parliament, and two members of the European Commission. Whatever misgivings there had been about Giscard's appointment they were dispelled by his display of intellect and energy, and his pragmatic chairmanship spiced with occasional brinkmanship. A number of working groups were set up to discuss problematic issues in detail, supplemented by more private 'discussion circles' in which real rows could be had. Important as this working method was, it was only on the floor of the plenary that the presidency could divine whether or not a sufficient consensus had been reached. Often it was not. The Convention should be judged not only on the quality of the consensus achieved but on the raft of diagnoses and prescriptions it discarded.

The European Parliament had a good Convention. Its delegation readily understood Giscard's injunction to compromise. At the outset, many expected that the MEPs would be outmanoeuvred by national governments as the negotiations reached their climax and the hard bargains had to be struck. This did not happen. In fact, if anything the role of the MEPs became more vital in the last weeks of the Convention when crucial coalitions had to be formed on the floor of the plenary and in party caucus meetings, which were led by MEPs. While Giscard d'Estaing was understandably anxious to secure the consent of the national leaders (especially from the larger member states), he also knew that no consensus would be possible in the Convention without the active involvement of MEPs. From the outset Giscard and the European Parliament delegation were united in their hostility to producing a mere options paper for the IGC. They both wanted, and eventually got, a single draft constitution against the expectations of most representatives of governments and national parliaments.

Penelope

The European Commission had a less happy Convention. Two of its top members, Michel Barnier and Antonio Vitorino, were very effective members of the Convention praesidium, but the college as a whole, deprived of its sole right of initiative, seemed disoriented. Relations between the Commission President, Romano Prodi, and Giscard d'Estaing were never good, and descended to rock-bottom when the existence of a secret draft of the new constitution was leaked to the press. This was the product of a working party established by Prodi and led by François Lamoureux, a former adviser to Jacques Delors. Nicknamed 'Penelope', the draft was published in December 2002 as a 'feasibility study [which] does not necessarily represent the views of the European Commission'.[11] Barnier and Vitorino were embarrassed; other members of the Convention affronted; and Giscard enraged.

Because its sudden appearance had been explosive, it was difficult for the Convention to deal with the Penelope project. Yet Penelope was an important initiative with an afterlife, and is worth close study. It represents the most federalist constitutional initiative since Altiero Spinelli's remarkable (but incomplete and unaccomplished) draft Treaty on European Union which had been adopted by the European Parliament in February 1984.[12] Drawing on the Spinelli draft treaty and on a more recent study from the European University at Florence, Penelope was a complete reworking of the current EU treaties.[13] It is unashamedly a constitutional text, with a hierarchy laid down of principles, objectives, rights and policies. The 'Community method' is generalised whereby the Commission initiates and decisions are taken jointly by the Council and Parliament. While qualified majority voting (QMV) becomes the norm for the Council, Penelope protected the practice whereby unanimity in the Council is required to overturn a Commission proposal. The only exception to QMV concerned the decision to admit a new member state, which remained to be taken by unanimity.

While Penelope claimed to work *au droit constant* – in other words, making no substantive changes to existing EU law – it dropped the three-tier classification of competences favoured by the Convention (exclusive, shared, supplementary), and in doing so it implicitly enlarged the general competence of the Union to act over a wider range of issues. Three types of policy making are envisaged: 'principal policies', where the EU is the chief actor; 'flanking policies', where the EU coordinates and makes convergent national policies but does not sup-

---

11 *Constitution of the European Union: contribution to a preliminary draft*, Working Document, European Commission, 4 December 2002. 'Penelope' was the name of Lamoureux's yacht.
12 http://www.eurotreaties.com/spinelli.pdf
13 European University Institute, *A Basic treaty for the European Union*, Report submitted on 15 May 2000 to the President of the European Commission, Florence.

plant the role of the states; and 'complementary actions' which support national policies without seeking to harmonise them. Penelope's principal policies involve economic and monetary union (EMU), the Common Agricultural Policy (CAP) and Common Fisheries Policy (CFP), internal market, competition, transport, atomic energy, and justice and home affairs; flanking policies include economic and social cohesion, social policy and employment, environment, R&D, consumer protection, trans-European networks and health; complementary actions are foreseen in education and training, culture, media, industrial competitiveness, civil protection and space policy. A clear distinction is drawn between the legislative functions of the Parliament and Council on the one hand and the executive function of the Commission on the other – although that executive function has to be shared with the Council for economic policy, external relations and police cooperation. A hierarchy of legal norms is proposed based on the intensity of the action required: the choices of instrument run between organic 'institutional laws', 'European laws' (to replace the current regulations, directives and framework decisions), executive 'decisions' of the Commission or Council, and 'recommendations' of the Commission or Council.

Penelope made a bold attempt to improve the language of the treaties. This required modernisation of terminology, suppression of repetition, and the application of a healthy dose of sub-editing to forty years' worth of accumulated legalese – much of which had been crafted to mask political ambiguity.[14] The Convention did its best to follow the textual simplification and structural rationalisation presented by Penelope. However, the compromise that was eventually deemed necessary to convert the defeated Constitutional Treaty into the more acceptable Treaty of Lisbon sent the simplification exercise into reverse. After 2005, obscurantism and obfuscation were the order of the day: even the fusion into one new treaty of the two current treaties, the Treaty on European Union and the Treaty establishing the European Community, a fusion which the Convention executed with panache, was abandoned.

---

14 Penelope also devised five subsidiary Additional Acts to the main text, concerning (1) defence, (2) atomic energy, (3) association of overseas countries and territories, (4) supplementary institutional provisions, and (5) territorial application, protocols, transitional and miscellaneous provisions.

The Constitutional Treaty

The Penelope episode was uncomfortable for the Commission, but it did not derail the Convention. What made the Convention robust, apart from the eclectic mix of personalities assembled, was its predominantly parliamentary character which allowed it to acquire a democratic dynamic of its own. Good ideas were allowed to surface. Painful as the experience was for many of the government representatives, having to argue their case in public was ultimately more legitimating than the secretive diplomacy to which they were accustomed in a classical IGC. The very public character of the Convention gave it constitutional gravity. When the Convention closed its doors on 10 July 2003, something remarkable had been achieved.[15]

The Convention's draft Treaty establishing a Constitution for Europe proposed a large pooling of national sovereignty upon the supranational authority of the Union. The Charter was made binding. Wider competences were conferred on the EU and significantly more powers were accorded the institutions. Constitutional checks and balances were reinforced. Part One of the Constitutional Treaty explains how the system of governance works, and how a country may join or leave the Union. Part Two comprises the Charter of Fundamental Rights. Part Three describes the common policies of the EU. Part Four contains some fairly straightforward general provisions and describes how the constitution may be revised in the future. In institutional terms, the main change – entirely in contradiction to Penelope – was the upgrading of the European Council to act as a counterweight to the European Commission and European Parliament. This reform was especially popular with the UK government which, having sought in the first instance to prevent the Convention taking place, tried continually to undermine it and, subsequently, to reduce the force of its proposals.[16]

The Convention came to recognise that there were issues of sovereign importance to member states that were not susceptible to the new style of open discourse it had established. Those questions related not so much to the balance of power between the states and the Union level

15   Draft Treaty establishing a Constitution for Europe (DCT). www.whi-berlin.eu/documents/draft_english.pdf

16   Alain Lamassoure MEP told the Convention that the difference between it and Philadelphia was that the Americans had solved the British problem before they began to draft their constitution.

of government, but to the balance of advantage among the states themselves. There was tension between the larger and smaller states, between the older and newer, and between the richer and poorer. Following the big enlargement of 2004, the phrase 'geographical balance' has entered the Union's lexicon.

In such circumstances, the Convention needed much collective wisdom to ensure success. One of the most necessary attributes was self-restraint. The Convention could – and did – stretch the mandate from Laeken, but there were clear limits to what it could do. That is why the Convention made no important proposals for the strengthening of the economic governance of the Union, and why today the Union is still beholden to the arrangements for economic and monetary union crafted at Maastricht a quarter of a century ago. Neither did the Convention tackle electoral reform of the European Parliament.

When Giscard presented the Convention's text to the European Council, the leaders received him politely, if nervously. They accepted the draft as 'a good basis' for starting the Intergovernmental Conference. The IGC opened with a formal session in Rome on 4 October 2003, but the bizarre chairmanship of Silvio Berlusconi caused it to flounder until the project was rescued by the Irish presidency in the first half of 2004. The final text was signed in an elaborate ceremony in the Campidoglio in Rome on 29 October.[17] It had been polished by the jurists and linguists, but the bulk of the Convention's draft survived into the Constitutional Treaty which was then dispatched to all member states for ratification.

In a referendum held on 29 May 2005, France voted No by 54.7% to 45.3%; three days later the Dutch followed suit by 61.5% to 38.5%. Europe's constitutional moment had been missed; the Constitutional Treaty was dead – but it was not quite buried. Under a (very) determined German presidency of the Council in the first half of 2007, the constitutional project was resurrected.[18] A new Intergovernmental Conference was opened, and the Lisbon treaty agreed. But controversy was not stilled.

This period of intensive constitution mongering which began at Laeken and ended in Lisbon grappled with the central dilemma of how to govern a Union in which, as the judges of the Bundesverfassungs-

17 Treaty establishing a Constitution for Europe (CT), OJ C 310, 16 December 2004.
18 See the Berlin Declaration of 19 March 2007, http://europa.eu/50/docs/berlin_declaration_en.pdf

gericht, the German Federal Constitutional Court, put it, there was only a 'limited willingness to unite'. The issues were fairly well exposed in the Laeken Declaration. Only the lack of genuine political consensus about the degree of integration that was necessary or desirable hampered the search for answers. Tension between those of a federalist persuasion, heirs to Monnet and Spinelli, and those of a nationalist bent, followers of De Gaulle and Thatcher, was never truly overcome. Every institutional prescription was a compromise – and not always a good one. Much of what was agreed was ambiguous, and nowhere is the ambiguity starker than in the decisions taken about the nature, composition, tasks and decision-making processes surrounding the exercise of executive authority in the Union.

The European Council

One of the most controversial issues was – and is – the role of the heads of government of the member states in relation to that of government ministers. This question had been unresolved since French President Valéry Giscard d'Estaing and German Chancellor Helmut Schmidt, with the blessing of Jean Monnet, had in 1974 transformed the occasional summit meetings of European Community leaders into more regular meetings of the European Council. By that time, European integration had advanced to become too important and central to the preoccupations of the national governments to be left only to ministers. The departure of General de Gaulle had made the experience of summit meetings at least tolerable and in some cases, notably at The Hague in 1969 and Paris in 1972, of historical significance to the advance of European integration. Summits also proved indispensable in moments of crisis, such as in 1973-74 when Europe was hit by its first oil shortages. Furthermore, it was deemed opportune to reinforce the European Council as a powerful intergovernmental anchor to the EU's system of governance at the same time as it was decided to allow direct elections by universal suffrage to the European Parliament.[19] The first direct elections took place in May 1979, and as expected the new-style MEPs immediately set to work to aggrandise the powers of their institution as a counterpoint to the intergovernmental European Council.

In principle, Giscard had favoured informal heads of government

---

19 Act concerning the Direct Election of the European Parliament by universal suffrage, 1976.

meetings – 'fireside chats' – where the leaders could discuss business without constraint (and without the European Commission). Fortunately, Roy Jenkins, President of the Commission from 1977-81 and almost the equal of Giscard in terms of self-esteem, asserted successfully the right of the Commission President to participate at meetings of the European Council, as well as at the G7 summits of the major industrialised countries. But in institutional terms the disjunction between European Council and Council of Ministers was a continual worry. Would ministers simply defer difficult decisions and push them upstairs for their bosses to deal with? Or would the heads of government interfere clumsily in the legislative processes which were more properly the preserve of the ministers in Council? And, above all, would individual heads of government faithfully accept collective responsibility for the actions of the European Council? On this, the omens were not good. Too often the presidency's conclusions of the European Council were unpicked or interpreted in very different (and rather nationalistic) terms at the simultaneous individual press conferences of the leaders held, usually late at night, at the close of every meeting. Once back home, as François Hollande and Matteo Renzi are discovering afresh, it proves very difficult to sell the strictures and prescriptions of the European Council, be they ever so correct, to hostile national parties and parliaments.

Penelope sought to resolve these problems by ceasing to regard the European Council as a separate body from the Council of Ministers but, rather, by treating it as the highest formation of the Council – albeit supplemented by the membership of the President of the European Commission. Contrary to the intentions of Penelope, however, the Convention decided to redefine and upgrade the role of the European Council. Maastricht had said, simply enough, that the European Council 'shall provide the Union with the necessary impetus for its development and shall define the general political guidelines thereof'.[20] The Convention draft replaced 'guidelines' with 'directions and priorities', gave it a 'permanent' chair who would not be a serving prime minister, and had it meet quarterly instead of twice a year.[21] It gave the European Council various important jobs to do, such as agreeing the financial perspectives and in steering common foreign and security policy (CFSP); but the Convention explicitly prohibited the European Council

---

20 Article 4 TEU. Penelope stuck with that minimalist formulation.

21 Article 20 DCT.

from exercising legislative functions, a constraint made in the logic of
its proposal to create a special Law Council (officially the 'Legislative
and General Affairs Council') which would deal with all law making
as well as prepare and follow up the meetings of the European Council.
The IGC on the Constitutional Treaty, for its part, discarded the idea
of the Law Council: it merely divided the agendas of meetings of the
Council of Ministers into legislative and non-legislative activities, the
former to deliberate and vote in public.[22] The governments were uncomfortable with the concept of the Law Council on two grounds. First,
it would have made the Council very obviously the second chamber
of the Union's legislature and less of an intergovernmental executive.
Second, the ministers who would attend the Law Council would have
to be super ministers within their own governments, rivalling the ministers of foreign affairs and acting effectively as deputy prime ministers. Such a reform might well improve the coherence of national
European policy as well as the efficacy of the General Affairs Council,
but in terms of the domestic politics of several member states it would
upset delicate balances and traditional hierarchies.

The Council of Ministers

As far as the powers of the Council of Ministers are concerned, Penelope suggested that, in addition to its legislative and budgetary functions, it would 'ensure the coordination of the Member States'
economic policies' and 'decide on measures provided for in regard to
the Union's action in the field of external relations and in the other
cases provided for by the Constitution'.[23] The Convention gave the
Council wider scope: 'The Council of Ministers shall, jointly with the
European Parliament, enact legislation, exercise the budgetary function
and carry out policy-making and coordinating functions, as laid down
in the Constitution'.[24] And it was the Convention's formulation which
is maintained in the Treaty of Lisbon.[25]

Given what we know today in the light of the crisis of European economic and monetary union, it is noteworthy that in none of the most recent three revisions which the treaty has been through (Convention

22 Article I-24 CT.
23 Article 43(1) Penelope.
24 Article 22(1) DCT.
25 Article 16(1) TEU.

draft, the Constitutional Treaty, the Lisbon treaty) do we see a really significant shift of competence in economic policy from the level of the states to the Union. Only Penelope proposed to make some significant adjustments: the Commission was to make 'proposals' and not merely 'recommendations' for the coordination of national economic policies, including the surveillance of excessive deficits – a suggestion unfortunately not followed by the Convention which chose to leave the responsibility for critical decisions about the euro in the hands of the Council.[26] According to Penelope, the Commission was to act as the EU's spokesman on exchange rate policy in international fora.[27] And a special formation of the Council was to be established for the eurozone, which in the Constitutional Treaty took on the appellation of Eurogroup.

The question of who should run the business of the Council and represent it diplomatically has always been contested. Giscard was programmed genetically to favour a presidential system for the European Council and, against the wishes of the Commission, he eventually got his way. The Convention also created the new full-time post of 'Union Minister for Foreign Affairs' – originally dubbed in the American style 'Secretary of the Union' – who, despite also being a Vice-President of the European Commission, would chair the Council of Ministers of Foreign Affairs. The other formations of the Council of Ministers would continue to be chaired by ministers of each government in turn enjoying, if that's the word, a six-month stint.

The system of rotating the presidency equally between states had worked well enough when there were only six members of the Union, and it conformed to the principles of international law. It can be admitted that the spectacle of a new member state taking its turn to 'lead' the Union still holds some attraction, at least for the first time of asking. Each head of state or government of the Council presidency is allowed an appearance in front of the plenary of the European Parliament, and such appearances are always diverting and often important occasions. Nevertheless, the rotating presidency of the Council has proved less successful over time as the widening scope of EU activity has come to involve many more government ministers in complex business in Brussels and Luxembourg and as enlargement

---

26 Compare, in particular, the relevant provisions concerning the excessive deficit procedure in Article 104 TEC, Article III-71(7) & (11) Penelope, Article III-76(7) & (9) DCT, and Article 126(9) & (13) TFEU.

27 Article III-104 Penelope.

lengthened the gap between one term at the job and the next. With the time gap now standing at fourteen years there can be no hope of carrying forward valuable administrative experience from one presidency to another. The smaller states have difficulty in fielding enough competent ministers or officials to undertake the onerous business of chairing the Council, in particular during the 'trialogue' negotiations and conciliation procedures with the Parliament that take place under the ordinary legislative procedure. Many incoming presidencies succumb to the temptation to publish unilateral and sometimes populist 'presidency programmes' which run counter to the treaty-based injunction to agree a multi-annual work programme on an inter-institutional basis – to say nothing of the annual legislative programme of the Commission.[28] National hype around incoming Council presidencies is at best a distraction from the routine effort to run things well on behalf of the EU as a collective, and at worst an opportunity for self-interest and special pleading.

In the Convention, Penelope ventured to propose that the six monthly system should be abolished and, instead, that each formation of the Council should elect its own chair for a period of one year on a meritocratic basis. Penelope kept the rotating six monthly presidency of the European Council, however, and on the same basis envisaged that the European affairs minister of that government would chair the General Affairs Council. Having considered alternatives, including the actual merger of the post of President of the Commission with that of President of the European Council, the Convention decided to introduce a full-time President of the European Council, who would not be a serving government leader, for a period of two and a half years (renewable once).[29] But it also decided to stick with the system of rotating chairs of the Council of Ministers, with the exception of the foreign ministers, a decision which was maintained under Lisbon.

The rather unstable situation with regard to the presidencies of the Union institutions is rendered even more complex by the emergence on the scene of the Eurogroup. The Convention proposed that the ministers of the eurozone should 'meet informally' under the chairmanship

28 Worse, the additional practice has evolved of three prospective presidencies cobbling together one impenetrable 'trio' programme.

29 In this, the term of office of the President of the European Council would mirror the term of the President of the European Parliament, who is elected by MEPs from amongst their number for a period of two and a half years, renewable once.

of one of their number elected for two and a half years.[30] Not all member states were happy about the creation of the Eurogroup which risked contradicting one of the Convention's favourite nostrums that there should be no new institutions created. As a compromise, the Eurogroup was established formally as an 'informal' body.

Flexibility clause

There was also a lively debate in the Convention about the future of the famous 'flexibility clause', which has been much used to extend the operation of the Union when unforeseen circumstances arose and the treaties had not provided the institutions with necessary powers, notably over enlargement, the introduction of the euro and the establishment of agencies. It is a clause regarded as suspect by those, in particular national parliamentarians of a eurosceptic tendency, who fear 'competence creep' by an ever centralising 'Brussels'. This suspicion is not entirely without foundation: the rapid accretion of EU agencies which outsource work on behalf of the Commission – at considerable cost and without close scrutiny – has been largely accomplished by the deployment of this clause. Nevertheless such flexibility as the provision afforded is useful to the Commission and Council whose executive authority, sometimes exercised jointly, has developed in an ad hoc way.

Under the original flexibility provision introduced in the Treaty of Rome, its use was restricted to achieving the objectives of the common market. Council decisions were taken by unanimity and the Parliament was merely consulted for its opinion. Penelope sought to broaden the scope of the clause to allow for 'new action' by the Union in order to 'attain one of its objectives in implementation of its policies'; Council would act in accordance with a reinforced quality majority, followed by the assent of Parliament, also acting by a reinforced majority. The Convention accepted the idea of the broader scope and of Parliament's assent, but stuck to unanimity in the Council. It also added two riders: first, that the attention of national parliaments would be drawn specifically to the use of the provision; and second, that the provision should not be used to harmonise national law in cases where the constitution excluded such

30 Protocol on the Euro Group, DCT. Penelope had made no special provision for a Eurogroup on the presumption that all member states were intent on joining the single currency and would do so.

harmonisation. Later, in its turn, Lisbon complicated the matter further by proscribing use of the article in common foreign and security policy, and by asserting that the provision should never be used to circumvent the delimitation of competences as prescribed by the treaty.[31] These legal qualifications have not in practice prevented subsequent controversy over the deployment of Article 352. Several national parliaments, including those of Germany, Denmark and the UK, have introduced stringent special procedures to check the use of the clause.

It may be noted, furthermore, that Penelope carried a new article allowing for the establishment of EU agencies to assist the Commission in the exercise of its executive function. These agencies, which would be delivered by a statute under an institutional law, were to carry out programme management or provide scientific expertise; they would also be empowered to take decisions on the application of EU law.[32] It may be regretted that the Convention did not adopt the idea of a statute for agencies, not least because the Convention's solution to the problem of the implementation of EU law, a question to which the Laeken Declaration had drawn special attention, continues to be problematic.

The European Commission

Clearly, in spite of the agreement reached at Lisbon, both the executive authority accorded to the Commission and its political accountability are still in contention. Under the Treaty of Rome, the Commission was tasked merely with ensuring 'the proper functioning of the common market'. It ensured that the treaty and the measures taken by the institutions were applied. It could formulate recommendations or deliver opinions, 'participate in the shaping of measures' taken by the Council and Parliament, and exercise implementing powers conferred on it by the Council.[33] Penelope, naturally, was more ambitious, adding to the Commission's tasks the right of initiative and to propose the political programme of the Union, to implement the budget, to 'give effect to the laws and acts of the Council', to manage programmes and negotiate international agreements, to take decisions in

31 Compare Article 235 (then 308) TEC, Article 33 Penelope, Article I-17 DCT and Article 352 TFEU.

32 Article 71 Penelope.

33 Article 211 TEC.

the cases provided for by the Constitution, to 'ensure that Union law is applied and determine infringements of it', and, finally, to issue recommendations and opinions.[34]

The Convention, after deliberation, retained for the Commission the general right to initiate legislation. It added:

> The European Commission shall promote the general European interest and take appropriate initiatives to that end. It shall ensure the application of the Constitution, and steps taken by the Institutions under the Constitution. It shall oversee the application of Union law under the control of the Court of Justice. It shall execute the budget and manage programmes. It shall exercise coordinating, executive and management functions, as laid down in the Constitution. With the exception of the common foreign and security policy, and other cases provided for in the Constitution, it shall ensure the Union's external representation. It shall initiate the Union's annual and multiannual programming with a view to achieving interinstitutional agreements.[35]

It is the Convention's text which was essentially adopted in the Constitutional Treaty and then carried forward to Lisbon.[36]

Yet what really is the European Commission? Is it, in accordance with nationalist discourse, a bunch of unelected bureaucrats? Or is it, as federalists would have it be, a post-national government in waiting, like a chrysalis? The fact is that the concept of the Commission is mutable, and it is not surprising to find that the manner of its appointment has therefore changed over time.

The original High Authority of the European Coal and Steel Community was composed of eight members appointed by the Council and a ninth (Jean Monnet) elected by the eight.[37] Their mandate was to 'exercise their functions in complete independence, in the general interest of the Community. In the fulfilment of their duties, they shall neither solicit nor accept instructions from any government or from any organization. They will abstain from all conduct incompatible with the supranational character of their functions'. The states agreed 'to respect this supranational character and to make no effort to influence the members of the High Authority in the execution of their duties'.[38]

34 Article 45 Penelope.

35 Article 25(1-2) DCT.

36 Article I-26 CT and Article 17(1-2) TEU respectively.

37 The original eight members of the High Authority included two each from Belgium and Germany.

38 Article 9 ECSC.

The supranational character of the High Authority was diluted somewhat when it was replaced by the Commission of the European Economic Community. The three large states, Germany, France and Italy, each obtained two Commissioners[39]. 'The Commission shall consist of nine members, who shall be chosen on the grounds of their general competence and whose independence is beyond doubt.' The size of the Commission could however be altered by the Council, acting unanimously, although no state could have more than two members.

> The members of the Commission shall, in the general interest of the Community, be completely independent in the performance of their duties. In the performance of these duties, they shall neither seek nor take instructions from any Government or from any other body. They shall refrain from any action incompatible with their duties. Each Member State undertakes to respect this principle and not to seek to influence the members of the Commission in the performance of their tasks.[40]

With charming simplicity, the Treaty of Rome said that the members of the Commission 'shall be appointed by common accord of the Governments of the Member States'.[41] The Treaty of Maastricht amended the system of appointment in a rather convoluted way to include a role for the Parliament. The governments were to nominate 'by common accord, after consulting the European Parliament, the person they intend to appoint as President of the Commission'. The governments, in consultation with the president-designate, would then 'nominate the other persons whom they intend to appoint as members of the Commission'. The whole team were then 'subject as a body to a vote of approval by the European Parliament', after which the new college would be 'appointed by common accord of the governments'.

The practice of having an unequal number of Commissioners continued without fuss until the 'big bang' enlargement of the Union in 2004 when, under the terms of the Treaty of Nice, each state was given one member of the Commission only. Nice also boosted the role of the President of the Commission in distributing portfolios in his college, and further elaborated the appointment system, as follows:

> The Council, meeting in the composition of Heads of State or Government and acting by a qualified majority, shall nominate the person it intends to

---

39 Later joined by the UK and Spain.
40 Article 157(1) & (2) TEC.
41 Article 158 TEC.

appoint as President of the Commission; the nomination shall be approved by the European Parliament.

The Council, acting by a qualified majority and by common accord with the nominee for President, shall adopt the list of the other persons whom it intends to appoint as Members of the Commission, drawn up in accordance with the proposals made by each Member State. The President and the other Members of the Commission thus nominated shall be subject as a body to a vote of approval by the European Parliament. After approval by the European Parliament, the President and the other Members of the Commission shall be appointed by the Council, acting by a qualified majority.[42]

Nice upgraded significantly the role of both the European Council and the European Parliament in the appointment of the Commission. But the idea that Commissioners did not represent their own states was increasingly fictional, and the decision to deprive the larger states from having two members of the college – who had usually been drawn from government and opposition parties – accentuated that trend.

Penelope, for her part, reversed the process by giving to MEPs, acting by a reinforced majority, the right to nominate the new president. The president-designate would then be confirmed by the European Council, also acting by reinforced QMV. The Convention did not follow Penelope but came up with its own solution, later adopted by both the Constitutional and then Lisbon treaties, in which the European Council nominates the presidential candidate 'taking into account the elections … and after having held the appropriate consultations'.[43] Parliament then *elects* (no longer *approves*) the new president. The Convention thus laid the constitutional basis for the *Spitzenkandidat* experiment of 2014, to which we return later.

The Convention made another striking proposal to reduce the size of the Commission by aiming for a college of only fifteen members, including the President and the High Representative, the EU's 'foreign minister'. The thirteen would be selected on the basis of equal rotation between the states in which the 'difference between the total number of terms of office held by nationals of any given pair of Member States may never be more than one'.[44] Subject to that system, the composi-

42 Article 214(2) TEC.

43 Article 17(7) TEU.

44 Article 25(3) DCT. Penelope merely proposed that there should be fewer Commissioners once the membership of the Union reached 28; an organic law was to devise the formula.

tion of each college would take into account demographic and geographical factors. Moreover, each state being one of the thirteen would have to put up three candidates, including one of each gender, from which the president-elect would then choose.[45] The remaining states would use the same system to put up candidates to become junior 'non-voting Commissioners'.

Although many members of the Convention retained doubts about the merit of having junior members of the Commission, a version of that formula survived the two subsequent IGCs and passed into the Lisbon treaty. What was dropped was the best part of the Convention's proposal, namely that the president-elect should be able to choose from a shortlist of national candidates. What was added was worse, namely an escape clause which allowed the European Council, acting unanimously, to escape from the obligation to implement the reduction of the size of the Commission (to two-thirds the number of member states).[46] Of course, the European Council chose so to resile at the first opportunity, under pressure from the jittery Irish, in June 2009. The result is that the Juncker Commission taking office in November 2014 has an extravagant and unnecessary twenty-eight members.

This long and complicated (and unfinished) story is worth the telling because it demonstrates how the Union can never quite make up its mind about the status of the Commission. To some, especially smaller and more eurosceptical states such as Ireland, the retention of 'their' Commissioner is a matter of national pride. Others wonder whether a college, say, with no French member would carry much credibility in France. And there is something to be said for all national traditions to be reflected in the college at the top level. Yet there is no doubt that the presence within the EU's system of governance of a second standing conference of official representatives of member states – there is already COREPER – weakens the Commission's ability to be, and to be seen to be, a genuinely impartial actor working in the common interest of all EU states and citizens.[47] A non-omnipotent government of twenty-eight members is already very large, and the prospect of future enlargement of the EU to new member states – or of the

45 Article 26(2) DCT.

46 Article 17(5) TEU.

47 COREPER is the standing committee of the Permanent Representatives of the member states, resident in Brussels.

break-up of current member states into component parts – poses a recognisable threat to the efficiency and seriousness of the college.

The balance of power in the Council and Parliament

The power game between the states is not played out exclusively in the matter of the Commission's composition. The voting system in the Council has also been a battleground that has been more forcefully contested as the size of the Union and the prevalence of QMV has grown. In a classic federal system one might suppose that a majority in the second chamber of the legislature would be reached by a vote of at least half the states representing at least half the population. Would that things were so simple in Europe.

The Treaty of Paris (establishing the European Coal and Steel Community) gave one vote to each of the six states, but for critical votes (including in the case of a draw) it weighted the vote of the states producing 20% of the total value of coal and steel. The Treaty of Rome gave four votes each to France, Italy and Germany, two each to Belgium and the Netherlands and one to Luxembourg. A normal majority on a Commission proposal was made of twelve out of the total of seventeen votes, a relatively high threshold of 70.6%. When a reinforced majority was required, four of the six states had to be in favour. By the time of Maastricht that threshold had crept up to 71.3%, with at least ten out of the fifteen states in favour where special legislative procedures were involved. The Nice IGC, faced with the prospect of the imminent admission of the new member states, instead of simplifying the system and lowering the threshold, introduced many new complications. The Nice QMV for the EU of fifteen states was kept at 71.3%, with at least two-thirds of the states in favour for a reinforced majority. However, any state could veto the decision if the majority of the states did not represent at least 62% of the total population of the Union. The Nice QMV for the EU of twenty-seven states was set at 258 votes to be cast by a majority of states out of 345, or 74.8%. After a robust protest by Guy Verhofstadt, the Belgian prime minister, a Declaration was added to the Treaty of Nice which sought to establish that at no stage in the accession of a new member state would the QMV threshold rise above 73.4% and that the blocking minority of one-third of states will be 'raised' to 91 votes. (If you are confused, dear reader, so were the heads of government.) It seems to have been the intention of the IGC to ensure that a blocking minority would always require the votes of three larger states plus one. Trading between states for votes lasted for many weary hours at Nice and the outcome was unfair and irrational.

Reunified Germany kept the same 29 votes as the now much smaller UK, France and Italy; Poland, with a smaller population, fought for and won the same votes as Spain (27); the Netherlands (13) gained one more than Belgium, which broke the parity they had enjoyed since the first days. Objectivity was in short supply at Nice.

In the light of the QMV fiasco at Nice, the Convention got to work. After much discussion, it settled for the simple formula for a majority to be formed of more than half the number of states representing three-fifths of the population for normal votes (and two-thirds of states representing three-fifths of the population for special procedures).[48] As might have been anticipated, the subsequent IGC raised the threshold of the number of states from 50% to 55% and pushed the population requirement up from 60% to 65%, while adding that a blocking minority must contain at least four states.[49] The Lisbon IGC further complicated matters, as was its wont, by declaring that for abnormal measures 72% of states would be required to form a majority. In addition, and largely to appease Poland, Lisbon postponed the introduction of the new system until 1 November 2014, and gifted the Council a probationary period (until 31 March 2017) when any single state could insist on a return to the Nice formula for a particularly contested vote.[50]

All these shenanigans were not the work of a Union of trustful member states. In this respect, the Treaty of Lisbon has certainly failed the Laeken injunction to 'bring citizens ... closer to the European design'.

A comparable controversy to voting weights in the Council persists with regard to seat apportionment in the European Parliament, to which we will return later. The two factors are, of course, connected. If states of one size lose out in a redistribution of seats in the Parliament, they will seek compensation in an adjusted system of voting in the Council, and vice versa. The danger is that arguments over the balance of advantage between states will obscure the larger goal which must lie behind the work of any future Convention and IGC: to rectify some less good features of the Lisbon settlement and to strengthen the Union's capacity to act efficiently, effectively and democratically.

In the next two chapters we look at how the Treaty of Lisbon seems to be working in practice.

---

48   Article 24 DCT. Penelope ducked the issue and left a solution to a yet to be defined organic law.
49   Article I-25 CT.
50   Article 16(4) TEU, Article 238(2) TFEU and Article 3, Protocol No. 36.

2.

RIDING THE CRISIS

During the lengthy gestation of the Lisbon treaty, the European Union enlarged from fifteen member states to twenty seven. Enlargement was a major achievement, but it posed a challenge to the EU institutions which had to adapt to a new and more complicated balance of power. This difficult adaptation coincided with division over the US-led invasion of Iraq in 2003; there was disappointment that Tony Blair's Labour government in the UK did not reverse its Conservative predecessor's opt-out from the euro; and the negotiation of the medium-term financial perspectives for the period 2007-13 proved as fraught as ever. The failure to ratify the Constitutional Treaty in 2005 was a huge blow to the EU's sense of purpose and unity. So the eventual and belated entry into force of the Lisbon treaty was tempered by a certain nervousness about the application of the new constitutional arrangements. Perhaps too much energy had been spent on ratification and too little effort accorded to the task of understanding and explaining the import of its provisions.

It scarcely needs to be said that the period since the Lisbon treaty came into force has been dominated by the consequences of the financial crisis. The European economy is now entering its eighth year of slump. Investment is down 20% on pre-crisis levels. Unemployment in many countries is stuck at unacceptably high levels, especially for the young. Europe's banks have stabilised from the worst moments of the financial crisis, but the debt crisis still seems intractable. Demand everywhere is down. If Europe is poorer, it is also less secure. The international scene is troubled, especially in the EU's own neighbour-hood: to the South there is turmoil across the Arab and wider Islamic world, and to the East, Russia, discarding any pretence at sharing the EU's values, has invaded Georgia and the Ukraine. In fact, it would be difficult to design a set of geopolitical circumstances less conducive to the smooth introduction of a complicated new EU treaty than those which actually prevailed, and prevail still.

Growth in EU GDP (Source: Eurostat)

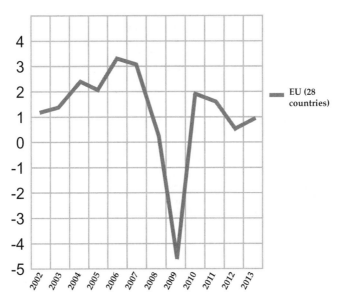

Coping with the financial crisis

To some extent, the financial and economic crisis has served to concentrate the collective mind. In the broader sense, the European Union under its new treaty has rather proved its worth when faced, as it was, with questions about the very survival of the euro. However, the evident necessity for a very large number of crisis management measures to correct the failure of the financial markets raised immediate doubts about how well suited the Treaty of Lisbon was to this task. The decision of its drafters to do nothing to reform the economic governance of the Union has come to be widely regretted.[51]

As the cohesion of the eurozone laboured under severe macro-economic imbalances, the original assumption that monetary union would lead inevitably to economic convergence was rudely dispelled. Eurozone states were individually issuing debts in a currency over which they had no control. The profligate use of cheap euros by the poorer states, and their avoidance of labour and market reform, allowed the disparity between the rich and poor countries of the eurozone to grow to intolerable proportions. As early as 2003, Germany and France chose to disregard the code of conduct on fiscal discipline – the Stability and Growth Pact – that every participating euro state had undertaken to respect. The pact, with a preventive and a corrective arm, intends to limit state deficits to 3% of GDP and public debt at or below or declining towards 60% GDP.[52] No executive authority existed at the EU level to bring the errant states back into line. Once the after-shock of the Anglo-American banking crash in 2007-08 reached mainland Europe, the new currency began to look very fragile. 'Grexit' (a term economic of characters on Twitter) entered the dictionary as shorthand for a Greek departure from the euro. This was not the occasional asymmetric shock always anticipated by economists but a full-on symmetrical assault for which the EU was totally ill-prepared. The Maastricht treaty's arrangements for EMU were brutally tested and found wanting.

An immediate target for collective action at the EU level was to correct the weak supervision of the financial markets and to strengthen capital requirements. In December 2009, the European Council agreed to set up a European Banking Authority, a European Insurance and Occupational Pensions Authority and a European Securities and Markets Authority. A European Systemic Risk Board was also established under the chairmanship of the European Central Bank (ECB). Enjoying its new empowerment courtesy of Lisbon, the European Parliament re-

51 In the vast literature on the crisis, see especially Philippe Legrain, *European Spring: Why our Economies and Politics are in a Mess – and How to Put Them Right*, 2014; David Marsh, *Europe's Deadlock: How the Euro Crisis Could Be Solved – and Why It Won't Happen*, 2013; and Stephen Pickford, Federico Steinberg & Miguel Otero-Iglesias, *How to Fix the Euro: Strengthening Economic Governance in Europe*, 2014.

52 Based on Articles 121 & 126 TFEU respectively, and Protocol No. 12. The Stability and Growth Pact was introduced in 1997, weakened in 2005 and strengthened in 2011.

sponded with efficiency, frequently strengthening the European content of the legislation. The new regulatory framework was made operational as soon as was possible.

A raft of legislation in the financial services sector was initiated by the Commission. Two main legal bases existed for the bulk of the new financial legislation: Article 114 of the Treaty on the Functioning of the European Union (TFEU) and Article 136. Article 114 provides for the approximation of laws for the purpose of the establishment and functioning of the internal market, with the exception of tax harmonisation. Unlike Article 114 which applies to all member states, Article 136 allows eurozone states to 'strengthen the coordination and surveillance of their budgetary discipline' and to set out economic policy guidelines in order to ensure the proper functioning of EMU.

When the economies of Greece and Ireland collapsed in 2010, rhetoric about solidarity had to be turned into rapid joint action at the EU level in order to restore financial stability. As bond yields continued to spread, innovatory bail-out mechanisms were created quickly. A European Financial Stabilisation Mechanism (EFSM) of €60bn was established under the authority of the Commission on the legal basis of Article 122(2) TFEU. This allows financial assistance to be granted from the EU budget to a member state when it is 'in difficulties or is seriously threatened by severe difficulties caused by natural disasters or exceptional occurrences beyond its control'. The UK, however, objected to the use of this provision to bail out a eurozone country, in the first case Greece. Whether the collapse of its economy was indeed beyond Greece's control is a moot point. In a self-denying ordinance, the European Council in December 2010 banned the further use of Article 122 for bail-out purposes.

Subsequent bail-outs have been arranged on an intergovernmental basis. The first such facility, for €440bn, called the European Financial Stability Fund (EFSF) was created just for the eurozone. Greece and Ireland were rescued first, followed by Portugal, Spain and Cyprus, plus a second bail-out for Greece.[53] The European Council launched a proposal for a permanent European Stability Mechanism (ESM) for the

---

53   To date since 2008, eurozone bail-outs from EU funds (excluding IMF and bilateral arrangements) amount to Cyprus €9bn, Greece €197.5bn, Ireland €40.9bn, Portugal €49.9bn, Spain €41.3bn. Under Article 143 TFEU, emergency balance of payments assistance has also been granted by the EU to non-euro members Hungary €5.5bn, Latvia €2.9bn, Romania €5bn.

eurozone, an innovation which was deemed to require, especially by Germany, a limited but important change to Article 136 TFEU. A third paragraph was added to the clause to read:

3. The Member States whose currency is the euro may establish a stability mechanism to be activated if indispensable to safeguard the stability of the euro area as a whole. The granting of any required financial assistance under the mechanism will be made subject to strict conditionality.

This was the second treaty amendment to be made according to the 'simplified revision procedure' introduced by the Lisbon treaty, with the collusion of the European Parliament and the ECB, and with the necessary unanimous agreement of all member states.[54] The ESM, with a loan facility of €500bn and a total credit capital of €700bn, takes over from the EFSM and the EFSF, and will apply to those states in need which meet the fiscal requirements imposed by the 'troika' made up of the Commission, the ECB and the IMF. Subject to strict conditionality, the ESM may give loans to support structural adjustments; it can purchase debt in both the primary and secondary markets, provide credit lines by way of precautionary assistance, and grant loans to governments which are forced to recapitalise banks. As and when a proper banking union is put in place with centralised supervision for the euro area banks, the ESM is empowered to recapitalise banks directly. In November 2012, after a challenge from an Irish MP called Thomas Pringle, the European Court of Justice found that the ESM and the manner of its inception were fully in line with EU law.[55] The ESM is up for review by 2018.

In parallel to these novel developments concerning bail-outs, secondary legislation continued to strengthen the EU dimension of economic governance with regard to fiscal discipline, macro-economic policies and structural reforms. In September 2010, the Commission launched its 'Six Pack' proposals aimed at reinforcing both the preventive and corrective arms of the Stability and Growth Pact. The Six Pack installed a new voting mechanism in the Council whereby a Commission proposal is deemed adopted unless a qualified majority of states can be assembled to block it. This method of 'reverse QMV' greatly

54 Article 48(6) TEU. The first, in 2010, was to adjust the size of the European Parliament elected in 2009 to conform to the Lisbon treaty. A third was the Protocol on the Irish 'guarantees', previously reported, finalised at the time of Croatia's accession treaty.
55 ECJ Case C-370/12 Pringle.

strengthened the power of the Commission, and had it been in place previously might possibly have prevented the breaching of the Stability and Growth Pact. However, even before the Six Pack had entered into force (December 2011), with applicability to all the member states, the Commission proposed another two laws under the legal base of Article 136 – inevitably dubbed the 'Two Pack' – which oblige the governments of the eurozone countries to present their annual national budgets in advance to the Commission for inspection and comment, and which also permit the Commission to propose to the Council that corrective action be taken by an errant state. To cope with these new duties, President Barroso upgraded the role of Olli Rehn, the Commissioner responsible for economic and monetary affairs. After a lengthy process of co-decision with the Parliament, the Two Pack entered into force in May 2013.[56]

The fiscal compact treaty

Not content with these measures at the level of secondary legislation, the German government, aware of the mood at the Federal Constitutional Court in Karlsruhe, had moved towards demanding another treaty change in order to reinforce fiscal discipline in terms of primary law – a quid pro quo for the creation of the ESM. The Euro Summit meeting (of eurozone member states – see below) in October 2011 agreed to consider 'limited Treaty changes'. Mario Draghi, President of the ECB, told the European Parliament (1 December) that he wanted a 'new fiscal compact' which would be a 'fundamental restatement of the fiscal rules together with the mutual fiscal commitments that euro area governments have made', in order that those commitments should become 'fully credible, individually and collectively'. Herman Van Rompuy, President of the European Council, took up the challenge. His target was a revision to Protocol No. 12 of the EU treaties on the excessive deficit procedure – a revision which could be undertaken by an abnormal procedure, namely a unanimous decision of the Council following consultation of the Parliament and the ECB.[57]

Under the coalition government which had taken office in London in May 2010, the UK eschewed all EU fiscal integration; indeed, it

---

56   For the complete EMU code of conduct see: http://ec.europa.eu/economy_finance/economic_governance/sgp/glossary_en.htm#code_of_conduct

57   Article 126(14) TFEU.

seemed barely to tolerate even its own participation in the 'European semester' under which the Commission makes recommendations to national governments about improvements to the productivity and competitiveness of their economies. Things were brought to a head by British Prime Minister David Cameron at the European Council meeting in December 2011: he refused point blank even to contemplate Van Rompuy's minimalist reforms, despite the fact that the UK would not be directly affected by the strengthening of the EU's coercive powers over the eurozone.[58] Cameron's bluff was called. The upshot was the Treaty on Stability, Coordination and Governance in the Economic and Monetary Union (TSCG), which was signed in March 2012 by all but the UK and the Czech Republic. In terms of constitutional law, this fiscal compact treaty is a hybrid: intergovernmental in nature but deploying the EU's institutions and envisioning its own incorporation into the Union's 'legal framework' within five years of its entry into force (that is, by January 2018). In that respect the treaties of Schengen (1985) and Prüm (2005), which were signed by an integrationist core group of EU member states (but left open to all), provided a precedent.[59] The fiscal compact treaty works only by way of close analogy with the EU treaties.

The Irish government submitted the new agreement nervously but successfully to a referendum on 31 May 2012; others ratified it through their national parliaments. In another important break with precedent surrounding EU treaties, the fiscal compact treaty was freed of the classic constraint of unanimous ratification: it was designed to enter into force once ratified by only twelve of the seventeen eurozone states. In any case, signatory states of the fiscal compact were enjoined to transpose the rules on balanced budgets into national law 'through provisions of binding force and permanent character, preferably constitutional' within one year of its entry into force.[60]

What are the main features of this treaty to which the British government so strongly objected? The signatories commit 'to strengthen the economic pillar of the economic and monetary union by adopting a set of rules intended to foster budgetary discipline through a fiscal

58 Protocol No. 15.

59 Schengen was wrapped up in the EU framework proper in the Treaty of Amsterdam, as was Prüm by Lisbon.

60 Article 3(2) TSCG.

compact, to strengthen the coordination of their economic policies and to improve the governance of the euro area'.[61] The fiscal compact treaty seeks to respect the institutional provisions of the EU treaties, including those connected to the European semester, as embellished by the Six Pack and Two Pack. The signatory states commit themselves to maintaining the revised Stability and Growth Pact and to accept automatic correction in cases of serious deviation. It obliges signatory states to install in their national laws a balanced budget rule with a lower deficit level of 0.5% of GDP. That is Angela Merkel's favoured *Schuldenbremse*, or 'debt brake'. The parties agree to support the positions taken by the Commission throughout the excessive deficit procedure. They stand ready to exploit the enhanced cooperation arrangements of the EU treaties 'on matters that are essential for the proper functioning of the euro area'.[62] And they promise to consult each other on all major economic reforms. The European Court of Justice (ECJ) will be used as a federal supreme court to settle disputes between the signatory states in accordance with an as yet unused provision of the original Treaty of Rome.[63]

With respect to governance methods, the treaty foresees regular Euro Summit meetings, including the Commission President, under a permanent chair who will report to the European Parliament after each meeting. Non-eurozone signatory states will be invited to these Euro Summits at least once a year.[64] The European Parliament and relevant national parliaments are expected to widen the scope of their interparliamentary cooperation to embrace the issues raised by the fiscal compact treaty. The status of the non-euro states in this new architecture is one of its vital characteristics. Many of the central European states rely heavily on banks established in eurozone countries, and Donald Tusk, as Polish prime minister, was right to insist that those countries which are genuine candidates to join the single currency have a vested interest in the resolution of the banking crisis and the design of the post-crisis eurozone architecture. Appointed to chair the Euro Summits from December 2014 alongside his new post as President of the European Council, in succession to Van Rompuy, Tusk is now in the optimal position to press his point.

61   Article 1(1) TSCG.
62   Article 10 TSCG.
63   Article 273 TFEU.
64   Article 12(5) TSCG.

In a precursor of the moves towards banking union from which the UK chose to exclude itself, an ambitious 'Euro-Plus Pact', designed to boost peer pressure among states in the matter of competitiveness and employment and in the stabilisation of their public finances, was signed in March 2011 not only by the euro states but also by Bulgaria, Denmark, Latvia, Lithuania, Poland and Romania.[65] The arrival on the scene of the Euro-Plus Pact and the fiscal compact treaty have divided the membership of the EU and are indicative of further division to come. The commitment to regularise the status of the fiscal compact treaty under EU law by 2018 presupposes that Britain's objections raised against it at conception will have disappeared at that stage.[66] Moreover, in March 2014 the new Czech government notified its partners of its intention to sign up to both the Euro-Plus Pact and the fiscal compact treaty, leaving the UK in more or less splendid isolation.

Prime Minister Cameron was received like a conquering hero on his return from Brussels after his vain attempt to veto the fiscal compact. In the House of Commons, the minority coalition partners, the Liberal Democrats, were mute and the Labour opposition dissembling. Bizarre as it may seem, the likelihood is that the UK under a Conservative government might never agree to the integration of the fiscal compact within the EU treaties. To make the point, the UK Permanent Representative to the EU wrote to the Council to 'reserve our position' on the fiscal compact.[67] The UK, he said, 'considers that it is important to ensure that no objectionable precedents are set. In this context, it notes that the EU institutions must only be used outside the EU Treaties with the consent of all Member States, and must respect the EU Treaties'.

'Genuine' economic and monetary union

In another attempt to bring new impetus to the drive for economic integration, Herman Van Rompuy presented a report to the European Council in June 2012 on the longer term consolidation of economic and

65 http://www.consilium.europa.eu/uedocs/cms_data/docs/pressdata/en/ec/120296.pdf
66 Article 16 TSCG.
67 Letter from Sir Jon Cunliffe to Uwe Corsepius, Secretary-General of the Council of the EU, 22 February 2012.

monetary union.[68] This was drafted in concert with José Manuel Barroso, President of the European Commission, Mario Draghi, President of the ECB, and Jean-Claude Juncker, President of the Eurogroup.

The first priority, said the four presidents, was to build a 'banking union' involving the centralised supervision of Europe's banks and new rules on capital requirements, and with a common method of bank resolution and deposit guarantees. The report was frank about the 'structural shortcomings in the institutional framework for financial stability'. A new integrated financial framework should involve a single European banking supervision system with ultimate authority resting at the EU level for the whole Union. Conferral of new powers on the ECB under Article 127(6) TFEU 'would be fully explored'. A European deposit insurance scheme would be introduced to re-insure national deposit guarantee schemes, and a European resolution scheme, funded by the banks, would oversee the winding down of non-viable institutions. A common resolution authority would control both these schemes, backed up, so far as the eurozone was concerned, by the fiscal backstop of the ESM.

Secondly, said the report, there should be decisive moves towards 'fiscal union'. In the short term this meant the Two Pack. In the medium term 'the issuance of common debt could be explored', involving 'the introduction of joint and several liabilities … as long as a robust framework for budgetary discipline and competitiveness is in place to avoid moral hazard and foster responsibility and compliance'. Progress towards the issuance of common debt should be phased according to criteria. 'A fully-fledged fiscal union would imply the development of a stronger capacity at the European level, capable to manage economic interdependences, and ultimately the development at the euro area level of a fiscal body, such as a treasury office. In addition, the appropriate role and functions of a central budget, including its articulation with national budgets, will have to be defined.'

Article 11 of the fiscal compact treaty, which provides for ex ante coordination of national structural reform, was to be applied with dispatch; the social dimension of EMU was to be given more prominence; and a series of mutually agreed contracts in the drive for competitiveness, backed up by solidarity mechanisms, were to be negotiated (mandatory for the eurozone, voluntary for the 'pre-ins'). Building on the European

68 http://ec.europa.eu/economy_finance/crisis/documents/131201_en.pdf

semester, the framework for policy coordination should be more enforceable, including in areas such as labour mobility and tax coordination, where common action against tax evasion is an urgent necessity.

Lastly, in a 'genuine EMU' there must be real political accountability at every level of decision making: this was 'political union'. More powers for national parliaments must be considered, as foreseen by Article 13 of the fiscal compact treaty:

> Decisions on national budgets are at the heart of Europe's parliamentary democracies. Moving towards more integrated fiscal and economic decision-making between countries will therefore require strong mechanisms for legitimate and accountable joint decision-making. Building public support for European-wide decisions with a far-reaching impact on the everyday lives of citizens is essential.

In July 2012, Mario Draghi famously announced that: 'Within our mandate, the ECB is ready to do whatever it takes to preserve the euro. And believe me, it will be enough'. If necessary, this would include Outright Monetary Transactions (OMT) to purchase government bonds on the secondary market. That autumn, the Commission sought to top Van Rompuy's report with its own more ambitious 'blueprint' of its own.[69] This put greater emphasis on the powers of the European Parliament and also fleshed out the longer term options, which included the creation of a special fiscal capacity for the eurozone, a redemption fund for the relief of excessive debt, and the issuance of 'stability' eurobonds. If President Barroso hoped to spark a lively debate on the triptych of banking union, fiscal union and political union, he was to be disappointed. Germany's reaction was particularly negative. Its partners had hardly to be reminded that the creation of a debt redemption fund or the issuance of joint liability eurobonds would breach Article 125 TFEU, commonly known as the 'no bail-out rule'. Making the ECB the lender of last resort would have required a change of its mandate on a scale that cannot be accommodated under the Lisbon treaty. At the prospect of treaty change, the leaders took fright at the dangers of opening up Pandora's Box. Came December, and faced with a follow-up report from the four presidents, the European Council chose to concentrate only on the banking union and to settle on a leisurely roadmap for the rest.[70] As Draghi's words of July had had a

69 COM(2012) 777.

70 http://www.consilium.europa.eu/uedocs/cms_Data/docs/pressdata/en/ec/134069.pdf

magical calming effect in the market place, the pressure to tackle the constitutional problems behind the debt crisis had also lessened.[71]

Progress was nevertheless maintained on the banking union. The Single Supervisory Mechanism (SSM), established under the authority of the ECB, was agreed in 2013.[72] The legislation for the Single Resolution Mechanism (SRM) was passed by the Parliament just in time before the May 2014 elections.[73] One of the sensitive issues in this complex legislation was how to cater for the interests of the non-euro states. The European Banking Authority has responsibility for writing the rule book common to all states, although it is the ECB through its arm's length supervisory and resolution bodies which is responsible for the enforcement of those rules. The question of differentiation and possible discrimination concerned the 'pre-ins', led by Poland, as well as the UK, which has no intention of joining the euro but does have an interest in maintaining those parts of the single market which it considers to be in its national interest. The solution reached for decision making within the Board of Supervisors of the European Banking Authority provides for a double majority – that is, a vote by simple majority or QMV among the eurozone states plus a simple majority among the non-euro states.[74] However, once there are only four or fewer non-euro states, the double majority system will disappear. Thus this deal, which was much trumpeted by British ministers as a safeguard of British national sovereignty, is of limited duration. The same double majority procedure was built into the SSM. However, British anxiety about 'caucusing' by eurozone states against the presumed interests of the City of London has not subsided; and it will be stirred up again once Lisbon's new system for voting in the Council, which gives the eurozone an inbuilt QMV, takes effect after its final introduction in November 2014.

When the ECB, via the Single Supervisory Mechanism, ran its first stress tests of 130 systemically important banks in 2014, twenty-five banks were found to be in need of further capitalisation, nine of them Italian. These stress tests, which should set a precedent, involved asset quality review and demanded more transparency of the sector. It could be that the Single Resolution Mechanism to close down bad banks will

---

71 These events are very well chronicled day by day in Wolfgang Munchau's www.eurointelligence.eu.

72 OJ L 287, 29-10-2013.

73 http://eur-lex.europa.eu/legal-content/EN/TXT/PDF/?uri=CELEX:32014R0806&from=EN

74 Article 44 of the EBA Regulation, OJ L 287, 29-10-2013.

scarcely be needed in practice unless deflation sets in and confounds even the more pessimistic forecasts. Yet the modalities of the executive decisions on the resolution of failed banks are highly sensitive and quite Byzantine. In the final SRM agreement, the Council will only be involved in these decisions at the express request of the Commission either to assess a criterion of public interest or to approve an adjustment in the use of the resolution fund. Because of the prohibitive character of the EU treaty when it comes to the pooling of public finance, the Single Resolution Fund has been established under a side agreement of an intergovernmental type that sets out the criteria for the transfer of funds and their progressive mutualisation.

At the time of writing, the banking union, although substantial, is still incomplete. At one level, the acquisition by the ECB of hefty new powers of prudential supervision over Europe's banking sector is impressive. The fact that Article 114 TFEU has been used as the legal base for much of the banking union architecture renders the new system an integral part of the single market project, even though the intergovernmental side agreement, outwith the EU framework, has been needed to create the Resolution Fund. That said, there is still no single deposit guarantee fund for the banks, credit institutions such as insurance other than banks are excluded, and the ESM cannot call on the resources of the ECB as the backstop it would need were a number of systemic European banks to go bust. In constitutional terms, the job is half done: the necessary resort by way of crisis management to non-EU legal methods and financial instruments leaves a situation which calls for eventual rectification if the integrity of the EU is not to be risked. In the wider picture, the four presidents have been unable to prosecute their original plan for a comprehensive roadmap to fiscal and political union. It now falls to Jean-Claude Juncker in his new capacity as Commission President to refresh the project. In this, he will certainly have the support of Draghi at the ECB, who has been anxious to insist that his own inventive approach to dealing with the crisis needs commensurately bold measures from the politicians. These indubitably include treaty change, whether Germany likes it or not. More incrementalism will not tackle the structural flaws of EMU.

Lessons for economic governance

During the negotiations on the regulatory framework for the financial sector the European Parliament played a vital part. As a result, Parliament has managed to acquire for itself important powers of scrutiny over the supervisory functions of the European Central Bank, even stretching to a role for MEPs in the appointment of the Chair of the Supervisory Board. Yet the need to enhance further the parliamentary accountability of the economic governance of the Union at both European and national level is now generally acknowledged.

The central problem, however, lies in the weakness not of parliament but of government. At the EU level almost no executive measure can be taken without the involvement of a rather large gallery of important people: the President of the Commission and his Vice-President responsible for economic and monetary affairs, the President of the ECB, the President of the European Council, the President of the Eurogroup, the president of the Eurogroup working group, the rotating president of the Council of Economic and Finance Ministers (Ecofin), the President of the ESM – and, too often, the Director General of the IMF. Executive authority in these matters is diffuse and opaque, when it needs to be quick, decisive and based on solid analysis. The clumsy 'bail-in' decision on Cyprus in March 2013 demonstrated the problem. It is not surprising that the financial markets and media complain that the EU's response to the crisis has always been a case of too little, too late. One does not need to be a cynic to know that peer pressure among government leaders does not work (and never will) as a method of EU governance. Moreover, at least under Van Rompuy, the European Council has been too easily tempted to give up on difficult matters whenever it has an electoral pretext for so doing in one or another member state. Its effort to tighten the coordination of national economic policies has not only failed on its own merits – policies are not yet coordinated – but also in terms of the substance of policy – a return to growth is still elusive. Government by and on behalf of the European Council has not broken the link between sovereign and private debt, nor has it reduced borrowing costs for all; despite German entreaties, structural reforms are still resisted in the poorer parts of the eurozone. Ineluctably, logic points the way to a further pooling of national sovereignty in an economic government of the Union. And this requires treaty change.

For many national leaders the most difficult matter of all involves EU treaty change. The object lesson of Pandora is frequently called in aid of avoiding constitutional amendment. Certainly, much has been done to strengthen economic governance in the wake of the financial crisis under the terms of the Treaty of Lisbon, such as the granting of supervisory powers to the European Central Bank.[75]   Technically

75   Article 127(6) TFEU.

speaking, it may be possible to do more just for the eurozone without changing the treaties by using Article 136, coupled with Article 138 which lays down the procedure that has to be followed to secure a unified position for the euro states in the international monetary system. The 'flexibility clause', Article 352 TFEU, may also be utilised in conjunction with the enhanced cooperation provisions for the eurozone alone – if the UK were ever to agree. It may even be possible to reform the 'own resources' system of the Union by unanimity without resorting to treaty change: we will see how consensual (and how radical) are the proposals that will emerge from the high-level working group, chaired by Mario Monti, which is to report in 2016 on options for the reform of the EU's revenue system as part of a mid-term review of the current Multi-Annual Financial Framework (MFF), which runs from 2014-20.[76]

Nevertheless, the Union cannot ignore for much longer the need to consolidate in terms of primary law some of the fiscal measures introduced in extremis under secondary law, for instance in the Two Pack. As we have noted, the incorporation of the substance of the fiscal compact treaty into the Union framework is already pending, as is the review of the ESM. The introduction of a new fiscal capacity for the eurozone with revenue from EU taxes, the creation of a common redemption fund, the launch of a large eurobond market under the authority of the Commission, the establishment of a proper EU treasury facility – these items on the EU's medium term agenda cannot reasonably be initiated, and surely not accomplished, without treaty change. As we have seen, the Maastricht treaty prohibited bail-outs, either by the Union on behalf of a member state or by one member state on behalf of another.[77] The maintenance of such a blanket prohibition in the treaty serves to negate the goal of fiscal union, the essence of such a union being that EU citizens, in the guise of taxpayers, should share a proportion of their mutual debt burden in an act of solidarity.

The irony is that the EU today already has several characteristics of a transfer union. As well as the ongoing structural fund programmes, there are provisions for emergency aid, as already noted.[78] The creation of the ESM, and for that matter the SRM, although officially non-EU

76   Article 311 TFEU.

77   Article 125 TFEU.

78   Articles 122 & 143 TFEU.

instruments, gives the lie to the argument that fiscal transfers between member states can never happen. But the intergovernmental form of the ESM jeopardises the principle of solidarity within the Union. Permanent bail-outs on an intergovernmental basis imply a great loss of sovereignty for the debtor countries and the commensurate empowerment of the creditors. That is not a good way to design a democratic polity. In a true fiscal union, the European Commission would be enabled to make fiscal transfers within the eurozone in order to manage a financial crisis or to support a common economic policy, for instance by providing incentives for structural reforms in the labour and product markets and in legal and administrative modernisation.

The German government and parliament are quite correct to stress the need to avoid moral hazard and to apply strict conditions to any transfers of money from rich to poor countries. The best way to secure such guarantees is to establish a federal government whose job it would be to manage democratically the interests of the EU taxpayer. Most Germans, being well-used to federalism, know this instinctively. So does their constitutional court: the Bundesverfassungsgericht has made it clear on several occasions that, particularly with regard to budgetary questions, if European integration is to deepen it must be fully legitimated by a democratic process of constitutional change at EU and as necessary at national level. In its judgment approving the ESM treaty, the German judges emphasise the prime role of the Bundestag in budgetary matters: participation in the ESM has to be informed, quantified, rules-based and ultimately reversible.[79] Other supreme courts, including the European Court of Justice, are heavily influenced by the German court and are likely to uphold the same principles.

---

79 http://www.bverfg.de/pressemitteilungen/bvg14-023en.html

3. THE INSTITUTIONS ADJUST

Throughout the first five years of the life of the Treaty of Lisbon, the main thrust of EU law making, and certainly of its politics, was focussed on the financial crisis. There was less activity in other sectors, though not inactivity.

The European Parliament

Lisbon gave the European Parliament many wider powers of co-decision, particularly in the fields of agriculture and fisheries, and justice and home affairs. The two arms of the legislature, Parliament and Council, were faced with an agenda whereby a large number of pre-Lisbon measures had to be recast to reflect new legal bases under more democratic legislative procedures. Specifically over the financial crisis, the European Parliament proved itself to be an effective law maker, with the Council accepting in whole or in part numerous amendments voted by MEPs. To expedite the work, there has been a sharp rise in the number of agreements reached at the first-reading stage of co-decision following informal 'trilogues' between Parliament, Council and Commission. Parliament facilitates informal techniques of law making by voting political resolutions which set out its negotiating position while stopping short of legislative resolutions that trigger the formal later stages of the ordinary legislative procedure.[80] More efficient law making and better standards of regulation are also encouraged by the deployment of 'delegated acts', whereby the Commission, under the *ex post* control of Parliament and Council has the power to adapt legislation on non-essential matters.[81] Understandably, MEPs show themselves to be less happy with the use of 'implementing acts', where it is left up to the member states to control the Commission's exercise of its powers of implementation.[82]

There is tension between the executive and Parliament concerning the negotiation and conclusion of international agreements. Here, MEPs have gained the power of assent to the EU's international treaties (outside foreign, security and defence policy), but they are dissatisfied with their limited right only to be informed about the progress of international negotiations, particularly in those areas such as trade and environment policy which require full co-decision between Parliament and Council for internal EU purposes. In the 2009-14 period, certain international negotiations conducted by the Commission and Council fell victim to Parliament's veto: bulk data transfer to the USA via passenger name records and the SWIFT system of financial transactions, the Anti-Counterfeiting Trade Agreement (ACTA), and a fisheries treaty with Morocco. Although most of these instruments eventually entered into force after modification, the European Parliament has become a powerful player in international trade policy – a factor more rapidly picked up by the US Administration than by some governments of EU member states. The EU's commercial negotiations with Israel are particularly prone to heavy criticism by MEPs, as are its 'pre-accession' funding of projects in Turkey and northern Cyprus. Parliament's muscle is certain to be felt in the Transatlantic Trade and Investment Partnership (TTIP) negotiations as counter-party to the US Congress.

The European Parliament has had to work hard not only to absorb its new Lisbon powers but also to adjust to its own sudden enlargement, including the addition of many new languages. Because of a certain discordance between political parties in West and East Europe, there has been a loosening of the ideological cohesion of Parliament's party political groups. Absenteeism, particularly by Italian and French

---

80   Article 294 TFEU.
81   Article 290 TFEU.
82   Article 291 TFEU.

deputies, is a problem. The huge turnover of MEPs at every election – more than 50% in both 2009 and 2014 – raises issues of continuity. The variable quality of its leadership makes the Parliament an awkward partner both for the Commission and for its co-legislator partner, the Council. While José Manuel Barroso worked hard to maintain constructive relations with MEPs, Parliament's relations with the Council have been more edgy. A number of important inter-institutional agreements between Parliament and Commission have not yet been extended to involve the Council.[83] An initiative to create a transparent register for lobbyists has proved only partly successful. No progress has been made in strengthening Parliament's right to establish committees of enquiry. The statute which governs the activities of the EU-level political parties loosely connected to the Parliamentary groups remains inadequate: the European parties cannot, for example, select or promote candidates for elections to the Parliament, nor can they engage in referendum campaigns on EU issues. Another point of contention between MEPs and the Council is the obligation on the Parliament, against its own better judgement, to meet twelve times a year in Strasbourg. In November 2013 Parliament resolved to seek a treaty change to resolve the Strasbourg question.[84]

Parliament has struggled to assert its influence over budgetary matters. EU finances are in a mess. The choreography of the annual budgetary cycle is depressingly familiar: the Council cuts the Commission's draft budget; Parliament tries to rescue the Commission; and meanwhile, in different orbit, the European Council piles on new goals and missions for the EU, most of which involve the spending of money. About 75% of the revenue for the budget – technically dubbed 'own resources' – comes from direct GNI contributions from national treasuries. The tight grip of national finance ministers over EU spending means the prevailing theme of the budgetary negotiations is not European added value, or cost efficiencies, or economies of scale but *juste retour* – which Margaret Thatcher translated as 'my money back'. Numerous and extraordinarily complicated rebates contribute to a democratic as well as a budgetary deficit. The European Parliament, which has no effective voice over the revenue side of the balance sheet, only reluctantly accepted a deal for the MFF 2014-20, which left the Union

83 See for example the Framework Agreement between Parliament and Commission, OJ L 304, 20-11-2010.
84 Protocol No. 6.

with a medium-term financial plan inadequate for its intended purpose. The Council succeeded in cutting the Commission's original proposal by 8%, with the consequence that the EU budget – totalling over €140bn per year – now has too little money to meet the growing expenditure commitments. Lisbon has not broken the cycle in which EU budgetary negotiations quickly descend to, and cannot then be raised from, the level of the lowest common denominator. The Parliament has not yet articulated arguments strong enough to persuade the Council to loosen the grip of national treasuries on the purse strings of the Union, even though a move towards genuine 'own resources' in terms of federal taxation would save national treasuries money.[85]

That said, and in general terms, an overall assessment of the Parliament after Lisbon must be positive. MEPs work hard to provide effective scrutiny of the Commission and the ECB. The European Parliament is an increasingly important political forum for debates with EU government and foreign leaders. It has passed the point in its evolution when it was a mere amalgam of national parliamentary traditions, and is fast becoming a post-national democratic success story capable of sustaining a proper government of Europe's new polity.

The Council

The impact of the Lisbon treaty on the Council has been as significant as that on the Parliament. For a start, there is the widening of the scope of the matters where qualified majority voting applies, for example to justice, home affairs, climate change policy, energy security and development aid. QMV is now the rule and not the exception, even if ministers and officials prefer to continue to act by consensus without bringing things to an actual vote. Unanimity is retained only for the most sensitive areas of national sovereignty: tax, social security, citizenship, languages, the seats of the institutions and the main lines of common foreign, security and defence policy. In addition, ministers have had to adapt to the treaty injunction that their legislative decisions must be taken in public – a duty which some of the rotating six monthly Council presidencies have been better at honouring than others.[86] The Council of Foreign Ministers has also had to come to terms

---

85   For a good start, however, see Jutta Haug, Alain Lamassoure & Guy Verhofstadt, *Europe for Growth: For a radical change in financing the EU*, 2011.
86   Article 16(8) TEU.

with the installation as its chair of the EU's High Representative for foreign affairs and security policy, who doubles as Vice-President of the Commission. And to their chagrin foreign ministers are now normally excluded from meetings of the European Council.

The most dramatic change imposed by Lisbon, indeed, was on the functioning of the European Council and, in particular, the introduction of a permanent chair who is not himself a serving government leader. In his five years of office, Herman Van Rompuy has used his powers to the full, presiding over as many as thirty-four meetings of the European Council, both formal and informal, as well as eight summits of the eurozone leaders. Most of these meetings, understandably, have been taken up with the financial crisis and its consequences. Many of its decisions have strayed into the legislative arena which, according to the treaty, is strictly speaking the preserve of the Council and Parliament. The troika of Commission, ECB and IMF, which imposes austerity programmes upon the crisis economies of the eurozone, has received its mandate from the European Council. While it is true that some difficult decisions have been ducked by the heads of government, in overall terms the European Council cannot be accused of having failed to live up to its treaty role of providing the EU with 'the necessary impetus for its development' and of defining its 'general political directions and priorities'.[87] Where Van Rompuy has been less assiduous is in relating to the European Parliament, to which, as he frequently avers, he is not accountable.[88] Nevertheless, as the European Council has accrued power, albeit in exceptional circumstances, the lack of parliamentary scrutiny of its performance has become more embarrassing. Some (but by no means all) government leaders maintain a dialogue with their own national parliaments about their visits to the European Council, but there is no effective obligation on leaders to take collective responsibility for the actions of their institution.

The last major institutional change wrought by the Lisbon treaty is the establishment of the European External Action Service. This was carved out of the external services of the Commission, a small part of

87   Article 15(1) TEU. For the best commentary on the affairs of the European Council, see Peter Ludlow in www.eurocomment.eu.
88   Article 15(6)(d) TEU. Herman Van Rompuy has been equally coy about responding to parliamentary written questions: he agrees to answer questions about his personal agenda, but not about the work or political positions of the European Council.

the Council secretariat and a growing number of national diplomats on secondment. Its first chief has been the High Representative, Catherine Ashton, who spent much of her time and energy – doubtless too much of each – on the internal organisation of the new hybrid structure. The EEAS is still an uncomfortable bureaucratic innovation, deserving of reassessment. Ashton has had some remarkable personal successes, notably in Kosovo and as the leader of the nuclear negotiations with Iran. But overall the Union's efforts to build a common foreign and security policy that leads rather than follows events have been underwhelming, a lacklustre performance that cannot be dissociated entirely from the institutional ways and means provided by the Lisbon treaty.

National parliaments

National parliaments appear to be disgruntled about the Lisbon treaty. This may be because the quickening pace and enhanced scale of European integration calls into question the capacity of national parliaments to hold their own governments properly to account for their actions in the EU arena.[89] If there is really a 'democratic deficit' in the European Union, as is often alleged, it cannot be just the fault of the EU institutions, but also that of national parliaments.

The Lisbon treaty usefully describes all the formal functions of national parliaments in relation to EU affairs.[90] These comprise being kept informed by the EU institutions, verifying respect for subsidiarity, the special monitoring of EU activities in justice and home affairs, participation in treaty revision and enlargement, and involvement in interparliamentary collaboration. National parliaments also have explicit powers of assent to changes in decision-making procedures that fall short of treaty revision, mainly involving a shift via a '*passerelle*', or bridging clause, from unanimity to QMV in the Council or from special legislative procedures to the ordinary legislative procedure. There is a general *passerelle* clause which is triggered by the European Council acting unanimously.[91] Specific *passerelles* allow for the adoption of QMV in foreign and security policy, family law, social policy, some re-

89 Article 10 TEU.
90 Article 12 TEU.
91 Article 48(7) TEU.

served items concerning environmental policy and energy supply, the MFF, and enhanced cooperation.[92] Either implicitly or explicitly, deployment of these *passerelle* clauses will require heads of government to get the by-your-leave of national parliaments. As we have noted, some national parliaments now insist on taking a vote to endorse the use of the mistrusted flexibility clause, Article 352.

Codifying the practice introduced informally by the Barroso Commission before Lisbon, Protocol No. 1 requires the Commission to communicate directly with national parliaments. Protocol No. 2 deals with the EU's compliance with the principle of subsidiarity. National parliaments are invited to assess the scale and effects of draft EU laws in areas of shared or supplementary competence in order to verify that the EU is the right level at which to take action. Parliaments can raise a reasoned objection to a draft law on the grounds of a breach of the principle of subsidiarity. The subsidiarity test means not only that EU decisions should be taken as close to the citizens as possible, but also that there must be proof of added value in reaching the intended objectives at Union level. The objectives of the draft law themselves are not, in the strictest sense, part of the test. Yet parliamentary scrutiny is bound to bear upon the scope and force of the intended law as made explicit in its drafting, as well as upon any unintended consequences. National parliaments need to calculate whether a proposed EU law might be excessively disruptive at the national level, creating disconcerting legal uncertainty and giving rise to significant potential for judicial conflict.

National parliaments have eight weeks to act to raise the alarm. Neither the Council nor European Parliament will take a formal position on the draft law until after the expiry of that period. If, within eight weeks, one third of national parliaments object, the Commission will maintain, amend or withdraw the draft, and give reasons for its decision.[93] This is called, in modish football parlance, the 'yellow card'. Thereafter, if a simple majority of national parliaments continues to object – the 'orange card', an innovation yet to be seen in football – the Commission refers the reasoned objection to the Council and Parliament, which will decide there and then whether to end the matter. In dealing with an orange card the Council will act abnormally by a 55%

---

92 Respectively, Articles 31(3) TEU and Articles 81(3), 153(2), 192(2), 312(2) and 333 TFEU.

93 Article 7, Protocol No. 2.

majority (without the population factor); Parliament will act by a simple majority. *In extremis*, national parliaments are also entitled to raise the 'red card' with the Court of Justice which shall adjudicate on the subsidiarity question.[94]

National parliaments are minded to coordinate their approach to reasoned opinions. The treaty clearly intends that the reasoned opinions should be either identical or at least similar in order to trigger the constitutional early warning mechanism. Were one parliament (say the Italian) to complain that the scale and effects of a draft law did not go far enough in a federal direction, and another parliament (say the British) to grumble that the same law went too far thereto, the Commission would be off the hook. Random or contradictory opinions or those that are not reasoned on the grounds of subsidiarity are unhelpful.

The Lisbon IGC successfully killed off a proposal from the Dutch parliament to allow a simple majority of national parliaments to block any legislative initiative. This revolutionary 'red card' would have pushed national parliaments into direct conflict with the federal European Parliament, raising the spectre of the development of a confederal legislative chamber composed of national MPs. The EU has had previous experience of a European Parliament made up of delegations of national parliamentarians. That system was abolished from 1979 onwards because MPs have domestic and not European mandates and have neither the time nor inclination to focus properly on EU affairs, because MPs are all elected in different states at different times and for different periods, and, ultimately, because the growing importance of the European dimension demands a more professional approach. Given the much greater complexity and sophistication required of EU law makers today than forty years ago, it beggars belief to think that a reincarnation of the old system could work. National MPs have a job to do in the EU – but it is not the same job as that of the MEP, who enjoys a direct popular mandate as an EU-level legislator. It is reactionary nonsense, peddled by eurosceptics, to pretend that the EU's twenty-eight national parliaments are a more pure expression of European democracy than that represented by the European Parliament and the Council of Ministers, acting jointly as a bicameral legislature.[95]

94   Article 8, Protocol No. 2.
95   Article 10(2) TEU.

So getting the balance right in EU affairs is important for national parliaments. Some parliaments focus on interrogating ministers on their way to and/or from meetings of the Council; others concentrate on sifting enormous piles of documents in order to influence government decisions; several do next to nothing. Whatever their individual style, all national parliaments meet up twice a year within COSAC, the conference of national parliamentary scrutiny committees which exchanges information and best practice. After Lisbon, the European Parliament has made an effort to encourage interparliamentary collaboration sector by sector. Relevant MEPs and MPs regularly combine on a systematic basis to monitor and debate the European semester, common foreign, security and defence matters, and the development of Europol and Eurojust. Other joint meetings of MPs and MEPs are organised from time to time.

To date, the yellow card has been waved only twice. The first occasion, in 2012, was aimed at the Commission's draft law which sought to regulate the use of collective action by organised labour across the internal borders of the single market.[96] This complaint was not accepted by the Commission on the grounds of subsidiarity which, fairly obviously because of the subject matter, had not been breached. But the Commission withdrew the proposal in any case on the understanding that it had no chance of passing through the legislature. The second complaint, in 2013, raised more substantive arguments against the proposal to establish a European Public Prosecutor's Office. The Commission again refused to amend or withdraw its proposal on the grounds of subsidiarity, but issued a lively riposte on the matter (which deserves reading).[97] At any rate, the early warning mechanism will work none the worse for being deployed infrequently and with discretion. On the evidence, the principle of subsidiarity seems to be well enough respected by the Commission and the legislature.[98]

National parliaments are ill-advised to be preoccupied with waving cards. The real significance of the early warning mechanism is not that it will be much used, but that it might lend itself to the development

96   The 'Monti II' regulation. COM(2012) 130.

97   COM(2013) 851.

98   At the time of writing, since the entry into force of Lisbon 486 draft laws have been sent to national parliaments. In response, the European Parliament has received 294 'reasoned opinions' and 1513 political 'contributions'.

of good governance in the EU by stimulating informed parliamentary scrutiny of EU affairs in general. The true objective is to aim for better regulation. National parliaments can make a significant contribution to achieving this goal by helping the EU institutions to monitor the effect of EU law once in place, by reflecting more regularly and politically upon the European integration process, and by working as a conduit between the federal institutions on the one hand and domestic media and public opinion on the other.

Electoral reform and *spitzenkandidaten*

The European Parliament has been attempting without success to reform its own electoral procedure. Declining turnout at each five-year election – from 62% in 1979 to a bit above 43% in 2009 and a bit below in 2014 – causes concern. An election campaign with more of a genuine European dimension would help, it is argued, to galvanise the electorate and the media. Twenty-eight separate national campaigns, run by national political parties at the lowest possible cost, with their main aim being to recover from or prepare for the next national parliamentary election, do not do justice to the more mature and powerful body that the European Parliament has become. The citizen is cheated and the assembly is diminished.

A second anxiety has been raised concerning the composition of the European Parliament. In a landmark judgment about the constitutionality of the Lisbon treaty, the German Federal Constitutional Court cast doubt on the legitimacy of a parliament whose members are not elected by a uniform system.[99] In their *obiter dicta*, the Karlsruhe judges observed that a German MEP represented as many as twelve times the number of people as a Maltese MEP. They pointed out that the change made by the Lisbon treaty to the mandate of MEPs – becoming 'representatives of the Union's citizens' rather than, as previously, 'representatives of the peoples of the States' – was flatly contradicted by the fact that seats were still apportioned entirely per member state.[100] Moreover, the Bundesverfassungsgericht did not seem much impressed by the concept of 'degressive proportionality', which is the EU treaty principle underlying the current composition of the European Parliament

---

99   BVerfG, 2 BvE 2/08, op cit, paras 273-288.
100 Article 14(2) TEU and Article 189 TEC, respectively.

PANDORA, PENELOPE, POLITY

(and a perfectly sound federalist concept which, as federal judges, they might well have been expected to uphold). Nevertheless, the German court was right to raise the issue. Over the years, decisions on the apportionment of seats in the European Parliament between EU states have been haphazard, unfair and inexplicable. Seats have been traded between states, usually in the last hours of an IGC, to square more important deals. The 2009-14 Parliament was therefore entitled to try to reach agreement on an arithmetical formula for the distribution of seats which would have been durable, transparent and equitable.[101] The attempt was frustrated by the opposition of MEPs who feared losing their seats and their pensions, but useful groundwork has been done. We return to this in Chapter 6.

In parallel to the exercise on the composition of the House, an ambitious attempt was made to create, in advance of the 2014 elections, a new pan-European constituency for which a certain number of MEPs could be elected from transnational lists.[102] The objective behind this proposal was to galvanise the EU level political parties into becoming proper campaigning organisations. It would also have gone some way to assuage the grumbling from Karlsruhe about the non-proportional composition of the Parliament. But the proposal proved to be too ambitious for the plenary to accept. Many MEPs, especially from Central Europe, still thought in terms of the primacy of national delegations. Eurosceptic opinion in Scandinavia and the UK was against such a federalist experiment. Others, informed by the dreadful example of Pandora's Box, especially in the Council, feared that the changes in primary law which transnational lists required would open up larger issues of treaty amendment.

Out of the failure to introduce more radical electoral reform of the Parliament, a proposal emerged that each European political party should nominate, in good time before the 2014 elections, a champion who would compete with rivals for votes and seats on a transnational basis. This was Parliament's interpretation of the logic of the new system introduced by Lisbon, which we discussed above, in which Parliament 'elects' the new President of the Commission.[103] Parliament's

101 See Geoffrey R. Grimmett et al, *The allocation between the EU Member States of the seats in the European Parliament*, European Parliament Studies PE432.760, 2011.
102 See Andrew Duff, *Post-national democracy and the reform of the European Parliament*, Notre Europe, 2011.
103 Article 17(7) TEU.

logic crept up on the heads of government, most of whom seemed blissfully unaware of what exactly they had signed up to at Lisbon. However, once the four mainstream political families of European People's Party, Socialists, Liberals and Greens had set in motion their own internal procedures to find their *spitzenkandidat*, there was no going back. For a number of weeks, the chosen party champions debated with each other in several EU countries. In the end, only the British Prime Minister David Cameron and the Hungarian Prime Minister Viktor Orban held out against the experiment in transnational democracy (the latter seemingly out of personal animosity to Juncker). But British bleating about the scandalous 'power grab' by the European Parliament backfired with those, notably the Germans, who actually rather respect the world's first directly-elected international parliament. In fact, the frantic British campaign against Jean-Claude Juncker on both personal and political grounds made it virtually certain that he would eventually be elected to succeed President Barroso – as indeed he was.

The political storm across Europe which surrounded Juncker's election vindicated those MEPs who had first invented the *spitzenkandidat* idea. Despite accusations, not least from Giscard, that *'les lobbyistes imprudents de Bruxelles'* had engineered a coup d'état, President Juncker now enjoys a dual legitimacy drawn from both Council and Parliament, as well as a high media profile. EU democracy has made a small but significant advance. The next phase of treaty revision, whenever it comes, will surely need to revisit the procedures for the election of the Commission President and his college, as the European Council already implied when it accepted the fait accompli of Juncker in 2014. It will also need to return to the matter of European Parliamentary electoral reform and seat apportionment. Experience suggests that it is nigh on impossible to get agreement on any single one of these desirable reforms in isolation: a wider constitutional package deal is required in which reform of the European Parliament can go hand in hand with reforms to the Council of Ministers as well as adjustments to the role of national parliaments. Only another Convention could assemble all the relevant stakeholders and convince them of the need for a comprehensive approach.

Constitutional interdependence

In its extensive judgment of June 2009 on the merits of the Treaty of Lisbon, the German Federal Constitutional Court stipulated certain limits to European integration.[104] In so far as the EU remains a *Staatenverbund* – a union of states – integration can proceed unless and until German statehood begins to be undermined. EU integration must be clearly delimited and revocable by the member states, and the principle of conferral of competences made explicit in the Lisbon treaty must be respected. The European Union derives its own autonomous constitutional order from the constitutions of its member states. Under these conditions, the transfer of national sovereignty is a 'reversible self-commitment' by the states, but the transfer nevertheless 'permits a shift of political rule' to the EU and 'political self-enhancement' by the EU. However, '[I]f in the process of European integration primary law is amended, or expansively interpreted by institutions, a constitutionally important tension will arise with the principle of conferral and with the individual Member State's constitutional responsibility for integration'. Especially sensitive areas where European integration needs to be carefully monitored and subject to strict application of the principles of democracy and subsidiarity are criminal law, the use of military force, basic fiscal decisions, the shape of the welfare state and family law, education and religion. Yet there is no pre-determined constraint on the transfer of any type of sovereign right to the EU. 'Political union means the joint exercise of public authority, including legislative authority, even reaching into the traditional core areas of the state's area of competence'. Whatever happens with the EU, it must be democratic in accordance with German norms. 'Increased integration may be unconstitutional if the level of democratic legitimation is not commensurate with the extent and the importance of supranational power'. Because the EU is not today a federal state, the Council is not a proportionally representative second chamber of the legislature but of equal states, 'the representative body of the masters of the Treaties'; nor does the composition of the European Parliament need to be strictly proportional because it is merely 'a representative body of the peoples in a supranational community, characterised as such by a limited willingness to unite'; and the Commission 'as a supranational, special body … need not extensively fulfil the conditions of a government that

104 BVerfG, 2 BvE 2/08, op cit, especially paras 207-272.

is fully accountable either to Parliament or to the majority decision of the electorate'.

It may be regretted that the German court underestimates the extent to which the constitutional order of the EU is a compromise between, on the one hand, the democratic principle of 'one man one vote', and, on the other, the international law principle of the equality of states. The lessons from Karlsruhe, however, are clear: first, the more federal the EU becomes, the more representative must be its institutions; and second, if the EU were to take the qualitative step from *Staatenverbund* to *Bundesstaat* – a federal state – Germany would have to change its own constitution, the *Grundgesetz* ('Basic Law').

The 2009 Lisbon judgment of the Bundesverfassungsgericht has to be studied closely, not least because it has a large influence on the development of constitutional jurisprudence in other national constitutional courts and in the European Court of Justice. As EU law is challenged increasingly in the courts, Europe's judiciary relies often on each other's relevant case-law. No future treaty change can expect to escape from judicial challenge, and the skill of national supreme courts needs to be well honed to deal with such cases either on their own or after reference to the ECJ for a preliminary ruling.[105] The Czech Constitutional Court in Brno, for example, made two masterful rulings on the Lisbon treaty in fraught political circumstances.[106] It found that the values and principles laid down in the treaty and the Charter of Fundamental Rights are wholly compatible with those enshrined in the Czech constitution. In so far as Czech state sovereignty is concerned, sovereignty is not an end in itself but is a means of fulfilling those values and principles. In due course, also under pressure from the court and after a change of political direction in Prague, the Czech Republic withdrew its earlier request to amend the Lisbon treaty by adding itself to the dubious British Protocol No. 30 on the Charter.[107]

The Karlsruhe court has a natural pre-eminence in these constitu-

---

105 Article 267 TFEU.

106 On 28 November 2008 and 3 November 2009. Poland's Constitutional Tribunal followed suit in November 2010.

107 The withdrawal of the Czech caveat on the Charter followed the issuing of a negative opinion from the European Parliament to the request from the European Council to open up the treaty for revision – the first time that MEPs had exercised their right to say no to treaty change, in accordance with Article 48(3) TEU.

tional matters, not only because it is the supreme court of a rather recent, as well as a fairly litigious, federal republic but also because of the emphasis which the *Grundgesetz* places on German integration within the European Union. Needless to add, the Lisbon judgment has stirred up much debate, not least in Germany itself among the academic community and in the Bundestag. It is perfectly in order to ask why the Federal Constitutional Court painted the limitations of Lisbon in such didactic, even peremptory terms. For many in the original Convention on the Future of Europe the goal was not at all to construct a unified, centralised federal state, but, rather, to reach towards a federal union of states and citizens – that is, moving beyond the classic *Staatenverbund* to a uniquely European association of integration – *Bundesvereinigung* – or, more completely, to a post-national *Föderale Union*. Such evolution necessitates that in certain respects the EU is analogous to a state: the Lisbon treaty continues that development by conferring on the Union, for example, legal personality in international law and exclusive competence in commercial policy. But the Lisbon treaty is also careful not to expunge the essential sovereign rights of the Union's member states – a safeguard whose integrity was acknowledged by the Bundesverfassungsgericht when it dismissed the complaints against Germany's ratification of the new treaty. However, the court also laid down strictures concerning the rights, duties and procedures of the Bundestag and Bundesrat with regard to the control of German government EU policy, and insisted on a toughening up thereof.[108] These measures included rights for a minority of MPs to raise the alarm on questions of subsidiarity.

Lisbon and after

Five years – especially five crisis years – is too soon to be definitive about the strengths and weaknesses of the Treaty of Lisbon, not least because some of its reforms have yet to bite, while others have been postponed. The new qualified majority voting system in the Council – basically, at least 65% of the population from 55% of the member states – was introduced only in November 2014.[109] The jurisdiction of the Court of Justice in the field of police cooperation and judicial cooper-

108 BVerfG, 2 BvE 2/08, op cit, especially paras 401-419.
109 Article 238(3) TFEU.

ation in criminal matters is not fully extended until 1 December 2014.[110] The EU's accession to the European Convention on Human Rights is still subject to complex negotiation under the shadow of a British veto.[111] None of the many *passerelle* clauses have as yet been deployed. Attempts at enhanced cooperation have not run smoothly, and face legal challenges, not least from the UK.[112] Even Lisbon's proposal to reduce the size of the new Commission has run into evasive action by the European Council, leaving the college bloated and at least some of its well-paid members grievously underemployed.[113]

One may safely conclude, however, that the Lisbon treaty is not the last word in the story of the Union's constitutional development. There is certainly no prevailing sense of settlement but, rather, of crisis management with further battles postponed. Lisbon's deficiencies relate mainly to the governance of the economic and monetary union and the impediments to fiscal union, but in terms of political institutions too, Lisbon should be seen as an important staging post rather than a final destination.

110 Article 10, Protocol No. 36.
111 Article 6(2) TEU.
112 Article 86 TFEU.
113 Article 17(5) TEU.

4. THE RISE OF REVISIONISM

One never has to wait too long in Europe for the Counter Reformation.

Indeed, we should not ignore the arguments advanced by the nationalists who take the view that European unification has either gone too far already and needs to be curtailed, or that European unification of the type crafted by the EU was neither necessary nor desirable in the first place. Nigel Farage of the United Kingdom Independence Party and Marine Le Pen of the Front National are clear enough that they wish to demolish the EU altogether, without putting anything else in its place apart from trading arrangements. Other types of eurosceptic, such as Alternativ fur Deutschland (AfD), want to scrap the single currency but stick with a previous, perhaps pre-Maastricht, version of the European Community. In Hungary Viktor Orban, continuing on his trajectory from liberal dissident to right-wing populist, makes speeches in which he compares 'Brussels' to the Kremlin. Revisionism is growing across Europe. In 2013 Beppe Grillo's Five Star Movement became the largest party in the Camera and threatens to make Italy ungovernable. Sweden's neo-Nazi party won 15% of the vote in national elections in September 2014. The AfD is polling regularly at more than 10% and UKIP at 15%. On the left, Syriza, the party of Alexis Tsipras, looks to be the largest party at the next elections in Greece.

#Brexit

In terms of revisionism, however, the United Kingdom is in a class of its own. Its Conservative Party, the party of Winston Churchill, the party which took Britain into the European Communities in 1973, has launched a renegotiation of the terms of British EU membership under the banner of 'reform'. In May 2010, only five months after the entry into force of the Lisbon treaty, the Tories returned to power in coalition with the Liberal Democrats. During the election campaign it was alleged that all the main political parties had reneged on a promise to hold a referendum on the new treaty – an allegation which held more than a grain of truth. British public opinion, deprived by opt-outs from enjoying the full experience of EU open borders and misled for years by untruthful media, was travelling fast in an anti-European direction. The coalition pact between the Conservatives and Liberal Democrats made an ill-judged lunge towards 'Brexit' by installing into Britain's fragile constitution the device of compulsory referenda whenever EU treaty change causes more powers to be passed from London to Brussels.[114]

Surfing the nationalist wave, Prime Minister Cameron gave a much-anticipated speech in January 2013 in which he called for a renegotiation of British terms of EU membership.[115] To overcome its problems, he said, the EU needs 'fundamental, far-reaching change'. Assailing 'sclerotic, ineffective decision making', Cameron called for a smaller Commission. He demanded more flexibility to accommodate the interests of Britain which will 'never embrace that goal' of much closer economic and political integration. 'We must not be weighed down by an insistence on a one size fits all approach which implies that all countries want the same level of integration. The fact is that they don't and we shouldn't assert that they do.' He recognised that the eurozone will need 'some big institutional changes', but insisted that the UK (and perhaps others) wanted changes too, 'to safeguard our interests and strengthen democratic legitimacy'. He attacked the EU treaties' commitment to 'ever closer union among the peoples of Europe', which 'has been consistently interpreted as applying not to the peoples but

---

114 EU Act July 2011.
115 https://www.gov.uk/government/speeches/eu-speech-at-bloomberg

rather to the states and institutions compounded by a European Court of Justice that has consistently supported greater centralisation'. Others might want to maintain that commitment, but for Britain 'it is not the objective'. A flexible EU means that 'power must be able to flow back to Member States, not just away from them. This was promised by European Leaders at Laeken a decade ago [sic]. It was put in the treaty. But the promise has never really been fulfilled'.

Turning to democracy, Cameron declared: 'There is not, in my view, a single European demos. It is national parliaments which are, and will remain, the true source of real democratic legitimacy and accountability in the EU'. The British people want the single market but are angered by excessive regulation, the intrusion of European rights law and by the fact they have not had a referendum. 'The result is that democratic consent for the EU in Britain is now wafer thin.' He promised a referendum, but not now:

> I don't believe that to make a decision at this moment is the right way forward, either for Britain or for Europe as a whole. A vote today between the status quo and leaving would be an entirely false choice. Now – while the EU is in flux, and when we don't know what the future holds and what sort of EU will emerge from this crisis is not the right time to make such a momentous decision about the future of our country. It is wrong to ask people whether to stay or go before we have had a chance to put the relationship right. How can we sensibly answer the question 'in or out' without being able to answer the most basic question: 'what is it exactly that we are choosing to be in or out of?'

The prime minister went on:

> At some stage in the next few years the EU will need to agree on Treaty change to make the changes needed for the long term future of the Euro and to entrench the diverse, competitive, democratically accountable Europe that we seek. I believe the best way to do this will be in a new Treaty so I add my voice to those who are already calling for this. My strong preference is to enact these changes for the entire EU, not just for Britain. But if there is no appetite for a new Treaty for us all then of course Britain should be ready to address the changes we need in a negotiation with our European partners.

The Foreign Secretary William Hague backed up his boss in a speech in Berlin in May 2013. Copying the original Dutch proposal, he argued bluntly that in a reform of the subsidiarity early warning mechanism national parliaments should be given the right to block EU legislation.

In July 2012 the UK government proudly announced a lengthy uni-lateral review of the EU's balance of competences, the outcome of which was intended to inform the renegotiation process.[116] A total of thirty-two reports were anticipated before the end of 2014. The conclusions of this bureaucratic exercise are reassuring for those who would wish Britain to remain a member of the EU, but they are equally illuminating about the extent and effects of Britain's numerous current derogations from the EU norm. The UK's semi-detachment stretches way beyond the single currency and banking union. It is not a member of the Schengen free travel area and has a complicated set of opt-outs from EU policy in justice and home affairs whose integration is much advanced by Lisbon. The UK secured for itself the right to opt out of all acts of the Union in the field of police cooperation and judicial co-operation in criminal matters.[117] In July 2013 the UK decided to exercise this right to remove itself en bloc from all pre-Lisbon legislation. Thereafter it applied to opt back into thirty-three measures, including the controversial European Arrest Warrant, to which the Commission has insisted on adding two others in the interests of safeguarding the practical operability and coherence of the *acquis*. There is no doubt that cross-border law enforcement suffers as a result of the British attitude, which is at best ambivalent and at worst hostile to the EU's efforts to create a real area of freedom, security and justice. At the same time, the Conservative Minister of Justice has announced his party's intention of clipping the wings of the European Court of Human Rights at Strasbourg.[118] The UK is in danger of disrespecting the ECHR and, accordingly, of putting itself in breach both of the EU Treaty and the Charter of Fundamental Rights.[119]

In May 2014, by way of a further concession to UKIP and the Tory nationalists, and in a U-turn from his Bloomberg speech, David Cameron announced that, if still prime minister, he would now insist on the EU referendum taking place in 2017 regardless of whether a new treaty was ready but rather on the general question of 'In' or 'Out'. By adding that if his renegotiation is successful he will campaign to stay in the Union, Cameron infuriates his party and puzzles

---

116 https://www.gov.uk/review-of-the-balance-of-competences
117 Article 10, Protocol No. 36.
118 http://news.bbc.co.uk/2/shared/bsp/hi/pdfs/03_10_14_humanrights.pdf
119 Article 5 TEU and Articles 52 & 53 of the Charter.

his partners. There is very little detail provided on the terms of the British renegotiation. Cameron and his party want to abolish the time-honoured phrase 'ever closer union'; to return more powers to the Westminster Parliament; to strike down the Working Time Directive; and to stem the migration of EU citizens into the UK. All four issues are very problematic, and on the face of it cannot be intended or expected to garner support from Britain's EU partners. That much is clear. But more than that we do not know: the UK government has not yet presented a comprehensive catalogue of demands to its partners. Nor has Britain spelt out what form of new relationship it looks for at the other end of the renegotiation – for example, whether it would prefer the Norwegian, Swiss or Turkish model of association (or something else entirely). On the face of it, Britain's EU relations look set to deteriorate further: at the European Council meeting in October 2014 Cameron refused to pay an adjusted back-payment of the UK's GNI contribution to the EU budget.

Dutch disillusion

The tide of British nationalism is watched with amazement elsewhere in Europe, and nowhere more closely than in Holland. As in the UK, Dutch public opinion has driven almost the entire political class to become eurosceptic. The referendum of 2005, which so decisively killed off the Constitutional Treaty, saw the mainstream pro-European parties firmly on the defensive. Come the financial crisis, almost scuppering the euro, the Netherlands adopted an even more eurosceptical position. The prospect of having to bail out impoverished, lazy and faintly corrupt Mediterranean Europe appals Dutch taxpayers. Although the right-wing PVV and the left-wing Socialist Party were effectively excluded from government after the 2012 elections, the governing coalition lives in fear that whatever happens next in Europe will amplify the nationalist voice. In order to show off their new eurosceptic credentials, Prime Minister Mark Rutte and Foreign Minister Frans Timmermans announced a major 'subsidiarity review' of Dutch EU policy – provoking comparisons with the UK's home-grown 'competence review'.

The result of the review, announced in June 2013, is instructive.[120]

---

120 http://www.government.nl/news/2013/06/21/european-where-necessary-national-where-possible.html

It adopts an overwhelmingly negative tone about the EU as a whole and especially about the European Commission of José Manuel Barroso. The Dutch government:

> is convinced that the time of an 'ever closer union' in every possible policy area is behind us – as the result of the 2005 referendum on the Constitutional Treaty made clear, the Dutch people were, and still are, discontented with a Union that is continually expanding its scope, as if this were a goal in itself.

The government therefore threatens to take a strictly limited view of the competences conferred on the EU under the treaty. The European Commission will be granted no latitude of interpretation of legal bases and will be discouraged from exercising its own political judgement. What the Netherlands wants is: 'a more modest, more sober but more effective EU, starting from the principle: "at European level only when necessary, at national level whenever possible"'.

The Dutch paper is not without its own inconsistencies. For example, looser EU directives are preferred to tighter regulation despite the fact that this can let member states less scrupulous than the Netherlands off the hook when it comes to the thorough implementation of EU law. No fewer than fifty-four specific points are listed 'for action'. Many of these refer to draft measures currently subject to the ordinary legislative procedure (and therefore to be co-decided with the European Parliament). None are revolutionary. Some are depressing for those who wish to see the EU reach its full potential at home and abroad. The review paints a picture of a functionalist EU, largely devoid of political ambition. No effort is made to discover economies of scale or cost-efficient, European added value: only the national and not the European side of the subsidiarity principle is observed. The main gripe is that EU law is disproportionate to the matter in hand.

Like the British, the Dutch cling to fiscal austerity: 'The EU budget should not grow faster than national budgets'. The government opposes the idea of a new fiscal capacity for the eurozone with counter-cyclical purposes: 'Economic stabilisation can best take place at national level'. Direct taxation remains 'a national prerogative'. The Common Consolidated Corporate Tax Base is a bad idea: as far as tax is concerned, the Netherlands 'seeks to preserve national freedom'. The Commission is blamed at the same time both for seeking to iron out differences in taxation by way of infringement proceedings and for not taking simultaneous action against all errant member states.

In some areas, such as family law or the telecoms package, previous Dutch governments are blamed for having agreed to things which this one regrets. In any case, the potential of the Lisbon treaty in the harmonisation of criminal law should not now be realised; nor should consular services be transferred to the EU level. The EU programme for school milk and fruit should be scrapped. The EU noise directive should not apply to Schiphol because the airport is too far away from other member states for its roar to have cross-border effects. EU environmental legislation in general has put 'too much of an emphasis on means (rather than ends)'. Bilateral agreements between states are a better instrument than EU law – for example, on tax approximation, flood risk management and tunnel safety. In other areas, such as CO_2 emissions, worldwide legislation would be better than EU law. In the field of social policy, the Open Method of Coordination – now discarded by most – is preferred to EU legislation: 'no attempts should be made to bring about further harmonisation of social security systems'.

Mercifully, perhaps, nothing is said in the Dutch document about common foreign, security and defence policy, trade policy, the CAP, CFP or overseas development. There is no systematic attempt to respond to the plans for banking union, stronger economic governance and fiscal union which shape the Brussels agenda. And, oddly, there is no word either on improving the Union's democratic accountability or on strengthening its global competitiveness. In fact, the Dutch government comes out against amending the treaties. In a press release (21 June 2013), Timmermans said:

> The government emphasises that it is not aiming at treaty change. The Netherlands fully accepts the existing distribution of competences. It is the division of tasks that it is aiming to discuss: is everything that the EU currently does really necessary?

Amid the Dutch disillusion, however, there is some useful pragmatic advice: better *ex ante* impact assessments and more *ex post* review of EU law. The Commission should be more sensitive as to how its proposals will work on the ground in each and every corner of the Union. A more proactive attitude should be adopted to adapt legislation to take into account judgments of the Court of Justice. The appointment of the new Commission in 2014 – which turns out, somewhat ironically, to include Frans Timmermans as First Vice-President responsible for policing subsidiarity and deregulation – should be used to re-assess priorities.

British Tory eurosceptics, slavering over their own unilateral review of EU competences and powers, are upset to see no specific Dutch attack on their unloved Working Time Directive – and no support for either opt-outs or treaty change. Nevertheless, despite their differences over the treaty change question, the British and Dutch governments have much in common – not least a barely concealed contempt for the European Parliament.

Pandora's Box

The financial crisis and economic downturn have left public opinion across Europe more generally disaffected and pessimistic. Eurobarometer surveys plot how the EU has become the target of facile blame – but the differences between countries are stark. At the two extremes in the most recent poll, 76% of Dutch preferred EU membership, against 36% of British.[121] More than two-thirds of EU citizens perceive the EU to be 'bureaucratic', and more than one half find it 'remote' and 'inefficient'. The overall unpopularity of the EU institutions has reached a record high, which explains why political parties, by and large, have ceased to be able or willing to sustain the European project, and why national parliaments continue to agitate against 'Brussels'. Few voices can now be heard speaking up for Europe. Even the European Parliament can no longer be guaranteed to drive the European project: the result of the elections in May 2014 has seen the nationalist and eurosceptic forces grow from 20% to 30% of MEPs.[122] One-third of French MEPs want to leave the euro.

The reaction to the rise of revisionism by the traditional 'pro-European' forces is fairly lame. In the UK, the campaign of the British pro-Europeans appears to be based on the argument that, by staying a member of the EU, British influence will be enhanced – an assertion which, though undeniably true, is far from the whole truth and evades most of the critical questions about Britain's future position in a more federal Europe. Other leaders talk more eloquently of the need for EU reform. The French President told the European Parliament (February 2013) that he wants a 'differentiated Europe' based on 'new European architecture'; but he can surely be expected to try to delay any conclusion to a treaty negotiation until after the end of his term of office in May 2017. The European left is in broad revolt against the EU economic orthodoxy, arguing, with some justification that rigid EU-imposed austerity has choked off growth and increased overall public

---

121 Standard Eurobarometer 81, Spring 2014.
122 Calculated to include the ECR, EFD and *Non-Inscrits* (unattached) on the right, and the GUE/NGL group on the left.

debt. Matteo Renzi casts himself firmly in the mould of reformer, but is short on specifics.

Before embarking on a new round of treaty change, the top priority of the new leadership of the institutions must be to try to restore public confidence in the EU. With the completion of the first stress tests run by the ECB, the supply side of the eurozone economy may be thought to have recovered from the worst of the crisis. Much now rests on the ability of Jean-Claude Juncker and Mario Draghi to stimulate demand and counter the slide to deflation. Unless and until the EU has restored its credibility for economic management it will hardly be possible for it to turn again to face its constitutional dilemmas.

At the start of a new period of constitutional reflection the first thing to do is to dispel the myth, so often trotted out, of Pandora's Box. The fact is that the lady opened her box some years ago. To cling to the Pandora cliché as if it is enough of a reason not to attempt further reform is to demonstrate helplessness unworthy of this generation of European leaders. Treaty change is difficult because European integration is not and cannot be simple. Treaty change has often been a driver of integration and, despite Pandora, the Union has usually emerged stronger from making the constitutional effort. It can do so again.

In the next chapter we will begin to ask ourselves what can be done in the next decade to escape from what the German judges called Europe's self-imposed 'limited willingness to unite'.

5.

AN AGENDA
FOR CHANGE

Notwithstanding that all EU treaties are constitutional, the Constitutional Treaty rejected in the French and Dutch referenda in 2005, and which provoked the ire of nationalist opinion, differed from its many predecessors in being advertised, even in its very title, as being overtly so. The granting to the Union of the appurtenances of statehood – the flag, the anthem, the motto, Europe Day – were a target for particular objection. Even the concept of common European citizenship, in fact invented first by the Maastricht treaty, was seen by the EU's opponents as an imposition upon and a threat to national citizenship. In Western Europe, at least, EU citizenship as an adjunct to the free movement of people throughout the internal market was suspected of encouraging the mass migration of cheap labour from the East.

Even federalists found difficulty with the argument that the Constitutional Treaty, while being a substantial improvement on the Treaty of Nice, was the answer to all of Europe's troubles. They searched in vain for signs that a constitutional patriotism was emerging in public opinion. The truth is that, for federalists, the Constitutional Treaty fell between two stools: on the one hand, pooling more national sovereignty at the European level; but, on the other, failing to establish a credible democratic way to govern the more powerful Union. The Constitutional Treaty advanced European integration by centralising power in the amorphous – and largely unreformed – EU institutions. And as things turned out, the technocratic character of the EU was actually accentuated by the expedient measures needed to respond to the financial crisis and economic recession. The federalist cause was in retreat even in the European Parliament. There was no chance that MEPs in this period could have supported the kind of thesis advanced by Altiero Spinelli in his draft treaty twenty-five years earlier. The large wave of enlargement after 2004 brought into the Parliament many deputies from Central Europe with no folk memory of the founding fathers of post-War Western Europe: national sovereignty just regained from Moscow was not going to be immediately thrown away in the direction of Brussels.

It was important therefore, and timely, that an initiative was launched in 2009 by Daniel Cohn-Bendit and Guy Verhofstadt to strengthen the cohesion of the federalist forces in the Parliament. Over a hundred MEPs signed up to the establishment of the Spinelli Group. In 2013 this cross-party 'intergroup' of European parliamentarians, aided by the Bertelsmann Stiftung, published a comprehensive draft treaty, entitled 'A Fundamental Law of the European Union'.[123] This elegant document sought to redress the balance of the debate about the future of Europe in a clear federalist direction. Refreshingly, it even decided to define federalism in the Preamble, thus:

> RESOLVED to continue the process of creating an ever closer union among the peoples of Europe by building a federal union deriving legitimacy from popular sovereignty in which no one level of government is subordinate to another but each is coordinate, ….

Likewise, the Spinelli Group replaces the phrase 'ever closer union' with 'federal union' in the first article of its proposed Fundamental Law. It seeks to establish a new federal polity which is effectively a re-foundation of the existing Union legitimised by both its states and its citizens. The resurrection of the 'f-word' comes as something of a shock. The Convention had avoided it scrupulously. Even Penelope was coy – deploying it only in the form of a curious quote from a Bruges speech by Giscard in 2002, when he said that the Union shall 'closely coordinate policies of the Member States and manage certain shared powers on a federal model'.[124]

The Fundamental Law is mindful of the need to protect the in-

---

123 The Spinelli Group & Bertelsmann Stiftung, *A Fundamental Law of the European Union*, 2013. http://www.spinelligroup.eu/article/fundamental-law-european-union (English and French versions).
124 Article 1(3) Penelope. No doubt this was inserted by Lamoureux to tease Giscard.

tegrity of the existing corpus of EU law, but its purpose is to provide a more robust constitutional framework within which Europe's governors and law makers would be enabled to make effective choices about the future direction of policy and the joint management of their affairs. Accordingly, under its provisions, the Union is amply equipped with such competences and its institutions with such powers as are needed to meet new challenges, primarily in fiscal and economic policy matters but also in the energy sector. The scope for opt-outs and derogations is minimised. States are expected to conform without equivocation to the emerging common foreign, security and defence policies of the Union as well as to the development of the area of freedom, security and justice.

The Fundamental Law of the Spinellists deserves close study. Alongside Penelope, it is surely an important source for the next Convention.

Fundamental Law: economic government

The main innovation of the Fundamental Law is to install an economic government to run the fiscal union, empowered not only to coordinate national economic policies but also to develop a common economic policy of its own.[125] The Spinelli Group takes membership of the euro as a given for all member states once the convergence criteria are met. Methods are proposed to closely associate the genuine 'pre-in' states which have joined the Exchange Rate Mechanism (ERM II) with the decisions of the eurozone by their participation to the maximum possible extent in meetings of the Eurogroup and Euro Summits. The euro states enjoy their own fiscal capacity for contra-cyclical purposes in addition to the general EU budget.

The government of the Union's financial and economic policies is placed squarely on the shoulders of the European Commission which, accordingly, acquires a proper treasury facility for the borrowing and lending of funds. A new post of Treasury Minister is created with the job of stabilising the Union's economy, allocating its resources and coordinating *ex ante* national economic policy reform plans. The Fundamental Law codifies in primary law the key elements of the Six Pack

125 Part IV FL.

and Two Pack legislation and the fiscal compact treaty. In order to ensure the establishment and the functioning of the internal market and to avoid distortion of competition, the Union is enabled to adopt acts in accordance with the ordinary legislative procedure in order to harmonise direct and indirect taxes.

While codifying the new supervisory powers of the European Central Bank as the cornerstone of the banking union, the Fundamental Law makes provision for the subsequent creation of a possible single EU financial services authority. It permits the progressive mutualisation of a portion of sovereign debt, and it lifts the prohibition, under certain conditions, on EU deficit financing. Specific legal bases are created for a common resolution mechanism and a deposit guarantee scheme. The European Parliament gains influence in the design of the employment and macro-economic policy guidelines, and both it and the relevant national parliament have powers to intervene in the application of the excessive debt and deficit procedures. A decision by the Commission declaring a state to be in excessive debt or deficit would be valid unless the Council could marshal substantial opposition to it.

The Fundamental Law transforms the Union's financial system by abolishing rigid *juste retour* and phasing out the system of direct budgetary GNI contributions from national treasuries.[126] Revenue levied by direct and indirect taxation would accrue directly to the EU. The unanimity rules for decisions on own resources and the multi-annual financial framework are scrapped. In a change to the annual budgetary procedure, the Council would be obliged to share with the Parliament an equal responsibility for concluding agreement.

Fundamental Law: institutional reform

The Fundamental Law aims at lifting the many prohibitions on the powers of the European Commission, European Parliament and European Court of Justice, rendering the system of governance more permissive and thus more capable. It seeks to reduce the number of main decision-making procedures to only two.[127] The first, for ordinary law making, stays more or less unchanged. The second is a special legisla-

126 Part III FL.
127 Articles 87 & 88 FL (ex-Article 294 TFEU).

tive procedure, replacing the numerous abnormal procedures of the current treaties that are subject to higher QMV thresholds in both Council and Parliament. Blocking minorities, emergency brakes and automatic accelerators are suppressed – all clever devices which may or may not have been intended ever to be used, but the inclusion of which in the Lisbon treaty smacks of ambivalence. Since legislative procedures with unanimous voting requirements are almost entirely abolished throughout the Fundamental Law, the sectoral bridging clauses (*passerelles*), which make it possible for the European Council to apply QMV in place of unanimity, lose their purpose and are deleted. Only the main *passerelle*, which allows the European Council to transfer matters decided in accordance with the special legislative procedure to the ordinary legislative procedure, as well as the *passerelle* to ease the decision-making procedures under enhanced cooperation are kept. QMV would apply to the flexibility clause, and a specific new legal base is created for EU agencies.

Following the logic of the Convention, the Fundamental Law merges Lisbon's two treaties into one document, and shortens the whole by reducing repetition and rearranging chapters in a more logical way. Likewise, the Fundamental Law discards many of the thirty-eight Protocols and sixty-five Declarations cluttering the Lisbon treaty, most of which are either tautological or seek to blunt the force and bend the interpretation of the original treaty.

The Fundamental Law is explicit that Parliament and Council form the legislature of the Union and that the Commission is its government.[128] Many of the executive powers now held by the Council are transferred to the Commission, subject to a possible recall by the legislature under a new procedure. The Fundamental Law presumes a smaller Commission, but it drops the conceit that the European Council, left to its own devices, could ever be able to agree on a formula for equal rotation. Instead, the president-elect of the Commission is empowered to choose the size and composition of his or her own college, subject to parliamentary hearings.[129]

The role of the European Council is adjusted to reduce the risk of tension and confusion between it and the Commission.[130] As in Pene-

128 Article 8(3) FL (ex-Article 10 TEU).
129 Article 15 FL (ex-Article 17 TEU).
130 Article 13 FL (ex-Article 15 TEU).

lope, the European Council is made more responsible than it is today for directing and coordinating the affairs of the Council of Ministers: the heads of government can even sit as the General Affairs Council. Reflecting its role as a legislative chamber, the rotating presidency of the Council of Ministers is replaced by the election in each formation of the Council of a chair for two and a half years. The president of Ecofin would also chair the Eurogroup.[131]

As far as the European Parliament is concerned, the Fundamental Law lays down comprehensive provisions for a pan-European constituency for which a certain number of deputies would be elected from transnational party lists.[132] Parliament also gains the power of co-decision with the Council on the vexed question of its own seat: each 'shall decide the location of their own seat, after having obtained the consent of the other'.[133] And it gets to vote both on the opening and closure of all international agreements, including those in the common foreign and security policy, and on the accession of a new member state.

While the Commission retains its powers to initiate EU laws, Parliament and Council gain the right to launch their own legislative proposals if the Commission declines to do their bidding. Parliament is enabled to push for the sacking of an individual Commissioner. In the case where MEPs decide to censure the whole Commission, Parliament must at the same time be able to elect a successor. If no agreement can be reached between Council and Parliament on the appointment of a new Commission, Parliament is dissolved and new elections are held.

Following Penelope, the Fundamental Law upgrades the status and content of European Union citizenship by giving rightful prominence to the Charter of Fundamental Rights, incorporated in full.[134] The rules to determine whether a state has breached fundamental rights are modified: QMV is introduced at the level of the European Council, and the European Parliament and the Court of Justice get to be involved in the decision.[135] Here the federalists seek to build on the operation of the Cooperation and Verification Mechanism introduced, after acces-

131 Article 14 FL (ex-Articles 16 TEU & 238 TFEU).
132 Article 12(3) FL (ex-Article 14 TEU) & Protocol No. 3 FL (ex-1976 Act).
133 Article 120(2) FL (ex-Article 341 TFEU).
134 Part II FL.
135 Article 133 FL (ex-Article 7 TEU).

sion, with respect to Bulgaria and Romania. Access to the ECJ is eased significantly for individuals directly and adversely affected by an EU act. The judicial scope of the Court is widened to embrace areas from which it is at present excluded, including the sensitive fields of internal and external security policy. The European Ombudsman would be enabled to defend citizens' rights more effectively, especially by gaining the right to refer cases of a breach of the Charter to the Court. The scope of the European Citizens Initiative is considerably widened by the Fundamental Law to include political agenda-setting. A legal base is established to extend the right of every EU citizen living in EU states other than their own to vote in all elections.

Fundamental Law: policy reform

Unlike Penelope, the Fundamental Law attempts a radical reform of the common policies of the Union.[136] While maintaining the basic free movement of goods, persons, services and capital, the Fundamental Law strengthens the defence of the European social models. Economic policy and the policies of the internal market are to be conducted in accordance with the goal of an open, highly competitive social market economy. The Union gains the competence to legislate on the fiscal component of free movement of labour, facilitating the portability of entitlements across national frontiers, and greater salience is afforded the promotion of employment and social protection. Lifting the prohibition on EU legislation on pay further strengthens the social dimension.

The EU is given a widened competence to legislate in the field of energy supply, aimed at creating a genuine internal market or 'energy union'.[137] In addition, the provisions of the Euratom treaty with respect to nuclear safety are incorporated. Both the Common Agricultural Policy and Common Fisheries Policy are modernised and disentangled from each other. A new competition authority is created at arm's length from the European Commission, in recognition of the fact that a more overtly political Commission should not also exercise directly quasi-judicial functions. Other policies, such as transport and R&D, are refreshed as necessary to reflect contemporary conditions. Environment

---

136 Part V FL.
137 Article 375 FL (ex-Article 194 TFEU).

policy takes on the additional task of combating climate change. Current prohibitions on the harmonisation of national laws in the field of justice and home affairs are lifted, raising the prospect of a more integrated European area of freedom, security and justice, including fully-fledged common asylum and immigration policies.

The Fundamental Law aligns common foreign and security policy more closely with the normal decision-making procedures, and enhances the role of the High Representative in the Commission.[138] She, assisted by two political deputies, continues to chair the Foreign Affairs Council and normally represents the Union in international fora. In CFSP the jurisdiction of the Court of Justice is extended, the scope of the flexibility clause is widened, and the use of enhanced cooperation is facilitated. The powers and accountability of the European Defence Agency are enhanced.

The Fundamental Law elevates into the provisions on enlargement the critical Copenhagen criteria on good governance which must apply to candidate states.[139] And an important new provision is suggested to complement the existing clause in the Lisbon treaty which obliges the Union to respect the domestic constitutional structures of the member states.[140] With Hungary rather in mind, the Spinelli Group proposes a new article to underline the constitutional interdependence of member states, thus:

> When undertaking constitutional reform at the national level, the States shall comply with their obligations as a state of the Union and pay due regard to the principles on which the Union is founded.[141]

How to change the treaty in future

There are two further proposals of major constitutional importance which make Penelope and the Fundamental Law stand out from earlier efforts at treaty reform. The first concerns the method of future treaty revision, and the second deals with the case where one or more member state fails to ratify an amended treaty.

The existing EU treaties insist on unanimity in the drafting of any

---

138 Part VIII FL.
139 Article 136 FL (ex-Article 49 TEU).
140 Article 4(2) TEU.
141 Article 4(4) FL (ex-Article 4 TEU).

treaty amendment and thereafter in the ratification process. On the face of it, it is bizarre that the European Union has encumbered itself with this constitutional straitjacket. Historically speaking, unanimity in constitutional matters is not very European.[142] No other international organisation or federal state, most of them established by British Europeans, have such inflexible methods of changing their statutes. The United States of America would never have come into being if each one of its thirteen original states had been able to wield a veto on the Constitution. The state of Bavaria has still not ratified the German Federal Basic Law under which it nevertheless operates quite happily. The EU, on the contrary, has faced near paralysis when one or other of its member states has stumbled over ratifying a treaty change. France and the UK almost failed to ratify Maastricht; Denmark had to renegotiate Maastricht after its first negative referendum; Ireland first rejected both Nice and Lisbon; France and Holland stymied the Constitutional Treaty.

Jean Monnet foresaw such difficulty. Indeed, his original Treaty of Paris (1951) adopted a form of treaty revision short of full unanimity. Institutional provisions of the European Coal and Steel Community, but not its central mission and competence, could be amended according to a relatively light procedure. Modifications could be proposed jointly by the High Authority and the Council acting by a five-sixths majority, which would then be submitted to the opinion of the Court. If the Court had no objections on constitutional grounds, the amendments would be transmitted to the Assembly where it would be ratified by a vote of three-quarters, if comprising two-thirds of the total membership.[143] Such flexibility was not to last. Under Dutch pressure, the Messina Conference which drafted the Treaty of Rome established the rigid formula by which treaty amendment has been governed since: 'common accord' for the IGC and ratification by all states in accordance with their own varied and uncoordinated constitutional requirements.[144]

Penelope adopted an ambitious if slightly convoluted form of treaty revision.[145] First, the European Council, acting by simple majority,

---

142 Even the Holy Roman Emperor and the Pope were (or are) elected by QMV.
143 Article 95 ECSC.
144 Article 236 TEC.
145 Article 101 Penelope.

would trigger the amendment process. The President of the European Parliament would then summon a Convention. The Convention would adopt a 'Recommendation' by a two-thirds majority of each of its three component parts (MEPs, national MPs and governments) 'provided that the total number of votes cast in favour in each of the three components represents three-quarters of the total membership of the Convention'. On the basis of the Recommendation, the Commission would draft the formal act and table it in the European Council. Amendments concerning the principles of the constitution and the Charter would be adopted by five-sixths of the heads of government and would enter into force after having been ratified by five-sixths of the states.[146] Amendments to the policies of the Union would be adopted by only three-quarters of the heads of government of states representing more than three-quarters of the total population. Entry into force would happen once three-quarters of the states had completed ratification.[147] Penelope's proposal is noteworthy for three reasons: for having eliminated completely the famous Intergovernmental Conference, for having the European Parliament take an automatic lead in the convening of the Convention, and in having one more and one less ponderous procedure dependent on the constitutional nature of the amendments in question.

In the event, as expected, Penelope's radical proposal was rejected by the Convention, although some elements survived.[148] In the draft Constitutional Treaty, the European Council, by simple majority, would trigger an IGC. Parliament would have to consent to a European Council decision not to call a Convention should one 'not be justified by the extent of the proposed amendments'. The Convention would work by consensus to make a recommendation to an IGC, which would itself operate according to traditional unanimous procedures. The IGC which drew up the Constitutional Treaty kept to the Convention's line, but added a new simplified procedure in which the internal policies of the Union could be amended by the European Council without the encumbrance of an IGC. Unanimity, of course, would still apply. The Treaty of Lisbon made no substantive change to these arrangements.[149]

The Spinelli Group, for its part, sticks with the Lisbon formula on

146 Ratification by 24 states in EU-28.
147 Ratification by 21 states in EU-28.
148 Article IV-7 DCT.
149 Article IV-445 CT & Article 48(6) TEU.

the Convention, in which the Convention reaches its conclusions by consensus; however, it proposes to modify the procedure for the Inter-governmental Conference, to allow treaty amendments to be agreed by only three-quarters of the states. The European Parliament would gain the right of assent to treaty changes as part of a ratification process in which amendments would enter into force once ratified by four-fifths of the states representing a majority of the EU population or if carried in a pan-EU referendum by a simple majority.[150]

Logic suggests, as Penelope and the Fundamental Law affirm, that the EU should modify its treaty amendment process to avoid the all too common situation in which one recalcitrant member state takes the rest hostage. But the radical nature of what is proposed should not be understated: treaty change by qualified majority, even leaping very high thresholds, is a big step in a direction away from *Staatenverbund* towards *Föderale Union*.

Dealing with dissenters

The question of what to do if the unanimous ratification exercise is thwarted has never been satisfactorily addressed by the EU's consti-tution mongers. Lisbon says meekly:

> If, two years after the signature of a treaty amending the Treaties, four fifths of the Member States have ratified it and one or more Member States have encountered difficulties in proceeding with ratification, the matter shall be referred to the European Council.[151]

What the European Council then does about the matter, aside from wringing its collective hands, is left to speculation, although it would have to react in the knowledge that the renegade state or states had the option of secession from the Union. For one of the most important in-novations of the Convention and the Constitutional Treaty, carried over into Lisbon, was the insertion of a new clause to allow for the orderly withdrawal of a state from membership.[152] The shadow of ultimate exit is therefore cast upon a rogue state which cannot or will not ratify treaty amendments to which its government has committed itself pre-viously in an IGC. The British problem makes this issue far from aca-

150 Article 135 FL (ex-Article 48 TEU). Ratification by 23 states in EU-28.
151 Article 48(5) TEU.
152 Article 59 DCT, Article I-60 CT, Article 50 TEU.

demic. But, from the academic point of view, it is interesting to note that, according to Penelope, withdrawal would not be an option that could be exercised freely at any time, but only at such a time as the Constitutional Treaty came to be revised.

Penelope was also inventive about how the present EU would change gear to be re-constituted on a federal basis. A separate document, an 'Agreement on its entry into force', was attached 'in order to propose a solution to the problem – almost inextricable in law – of the situation which arises if a State refuses to ratify the new Treaty establishing the Constitution'. In this side agreement the Lamoureux team proposed that each current member state commit itself in a solemn declaration to adopt the new constitution. If a state declined to do so, procedures for exit would commence. (An exiting state could claim to continue as a member of the European Economic Area along with Iceland, Norway and Liechtenstein.) According to Penelope, the new constitution would proceed on the proviso that three-quarters of the EU's current states made the solemn declaration. The constitution of the re-founded Union would enter into force once ratified by five-sixths of the states, at which point the laggard states could either sign the solemn declaration (and have the constitution imposed on them willy-nilly) or accept that their membership of the Union was deemed to have lapsed.

The Spinelli Group agreed with Penelope that although EU states cannot be forced against their will to take the federal step, they cannot, at the same time, be allowed an open-ended veto on the constitutional progress needed and desired by a large majority of their partners. Unlike Penelope, however, the Fundamental Law provides no mechanism for dealing with the complete rejection of the Fundamental Law by one or more of the twenty-eight current member states of the European Union. The assumption the federalists make is that any dissenting state would agree to settle for a new type of associate status. Were there to be no such agreement, expulsion is not an option, yet it would always be open in those unfortunate circumstances for the majority core group of integrationist states, presumably led by Germany, to leave the EU behind and to establish together a new federal polity. Under the terms of the 1969 Vienna Convention on the law of international treaties this rather melodramatic manoeuvre could be made even in the teeth of opposition from the UK.

The Fundamental Law therefore proposes the establishment of a new category of associate membership. This is the logical corollary of its proposal to lighten the procedures for treaty revision. Any member state which chooses not to join the more federal union will have the option of becoming an associate member.[153] The creation of what amounts to a category of junior membership is predicated on the insistence of the Spinelli Group that there should be much stronger government at the EU level to manage the multi-tier structure. According to the Fundamental Law, each associate state negotiates its own arrangement with the Commission, the latter acting on behalf of the core states. Both the rights and duties of the associate have to be stipulated. Continued allegiance to the Union's values is required, but political engagement in the Union's objectives is reduced. Partial participation in the internal market must not risk the operation of the market as a whole, and engagement with the EU's common foreign and security policy must not prejudice the cohesion or limit the scope of the Union's overall position. Participation in the EU institutions is limited, by invitation and on a consultative basis. However, associate states have to acknowledge the jurisdiction of the European Court of Justice, and might even appoint judges to the Court, who would sit only in cases where EU law is relevant to the associate state concerned.

The Fundamental Law conceives associate status as being not so different from the arrangements currently prevailing for the European Economic Area, but with a wider potential scope in legal and political terms, notably participation in the EU's common foreign, security and defence arrangements. Such an associate membership could cater for the needs of Norway, Iceland and Switzerland if they wished to improve on their present, different but uncomfortable relationships with the Union. It might also be a suitable lasting settlement for Turkey which has, to all intents and purposes, decided no longer to pursue its accession bid but which, nevertheless, desires and deserves a stable and structured relationship with the EU. Associate membership of the type envisaged by the Spinelli Group might offer a parking place for the United Kingdom, on either a short-stay or long-stay basis, should it choose to exercise its right not to remain a full member state.

Variable geometry

Under the enhanced cooperation clauses, first introduced under the Amsterdam treaty, a group of states can reinforce their integration in some carefully delineated circumstances in the area of non-exclusive

153 Article 137 and Protocol No 9 FL.

competences – but only 'as a last resort'.[154] The Convention and Lisbon kept and elaborated the Amsterdam clauses. Whereas the Fundamental Law caters for a more extensive use of enhanced cooperation, for example by dropping the caveat of 'last resort', Penelope abolishes the enhanced cooperation provisions almost entirely (allowing only sub-regional groupings such as Benelux, the Nordic Council and the Elysée treaty between France and Germany).[155] The authors of Penelope demand uniform commitment to full membership; the Spinelli Group endeavours to allow for a greater degree of variable geometry.

To date the only experiments in formal enhanced cooperation have concerned divorce law, the court system for European patents, the financial transaction tax and the European Public Prosecutor. Even the clustering of politically willing and militarily capable states in the defence sector, also provided for by Lisbon, seems a long way off.[156] There are nevertheless a few examples of pragmatic differentiation under the Lisbon structure: for example, not all EU states have joined or need to join Frontex or the European Defence Agency.[157] The Charter allows for states to enjoy their own higher standards of protection of fundamental rights.[158] And in social and environment policies, no member state is prevented from maintaining or introducing more stringent protective measures.[159]

The idea of a core group or *noyau dur* or *Kerneuropa* is not new.[160] Many advance it in the hope that a more differentiated EU would liberate everyone from the British problem; some have not noticed that the original axis between Paris and Bonn, and later Berlin, upon which so much was based, is no longer so reliable. Nationalists can be found not only in Britain but elsewhere as well, not least in France – and ignoring that fact by simply exaggerating the contrast between the UK and the rest of Europe will certainly put a very great strain on the efficacy and coherence of the EU institutions. Differentiation between

154 Articles 20 TEU and 326-334 TFEU.

155 Compare Article 20 TEU and Article 104 FL.

156 Articles 42(6) & 46 TEU.

157 Frontex is the EU's border control agency, and the EDA deals with arms procurement.

158 Article 53 Charter of Fundamental Rights.

159 Articles 153(4) & 193 TFEU, respectively.

160 Promoted most notably by Karl Lamers and Wolfgang Schauble in *Reflections on European Policy*, September 1994. Mitterrand's last prime minister, Edouard Balladur advocated three concentric circles.

states has its limits as an answer to the problem of policy divergence. Concentric circles look pretty but are simplistic. A plethora of inter-secting groups established in different policy sectors would need to be managed by a strong central government of a type that the EU does not possess. States cannot be allowed simply to pick and choose what they want from the EU and discard what they do not want. The point has been reached when yet more à la carte opt-outs and derogations would risk fracturing the cohesion of the *acquis communautaire*. Free-riding means disintegration. Dealing with differentiated integration is therefore delicate: while a multi-speed approach is a common sense solution to a situation in which some EU states are more capable of ad-vancing to achieve the objectives of integration than others – such as membership of the euro – a multi-tier approach, where states pursue variable objectives is an altogether different proposition.

While it is fairly straightforward to divide up the European Council and Council of Ministers from time to time into the Eurogroup forma-tion, that is not the case with the European Parliament, the European Commission or the European Court of Justice. MEPs, including British ones (whether they like it or not), represent all EU citizens. There is no precedent for depriving MEPs of their independent mandate to vote as they wish, on all manner of things, regardless of their direct rele-vance to the formal constituency of the individual deputy. As fiscal in-tegration of the eurozone deepens, there is a good argument for the creation of a new specialist committee or sub-committee in the Euro-pean Parliament that would devote itself to euro affairs. But to exclude non-eurozone MEPs from membership of such a committee would be a breach of the treaty. It would also be difficult to think of anything more discouraging for those MEPs from the genuine 'pre-ins' – those countries which are sincere in their efforts to meet the Maastricht con-vergence criteria in as timely a fashion as possible. Only as and when the EU moves to being able and willing to levy taxes specific to the tax-payers of the eurozone, would special voting arrangements be neces-sary in the European Parliament in order to mirror the separation at the level of the Council between euro and non-euro states. It would be wise for any new treaty to provide explicitly for such an eventuality without pre-empting its application.

The Commission and Court work best in a collegial fashion in the general interest of all states and citizens. Splitting them up is not a good idea. Discrimination against Commissioners or judges on the grounds of their non-eurozone nationality when decisions are taken that are only germane to the eurozone, apart from being of dubious legality, will scarcely contribute to the quality and coherence of the work of those institutions. Ultimately, there is something wrong if an organisation such as the European Union, whose mission is to unite, starts instead deliberately to foster division. It is not an accident that the EU treaties put great stress on the unity of its institutions and on the importance of working within the Union framework. The recent experience of the fiscal compact treaty which formally divides the UK from its partners is not a happy one for the Union, nor a durable one.

The gravity of the euro crisis, of course, has made some less squeamish about breaking up the Union into component parts in terms of primary law. In the past Valéry Giscard d'Estaing spoke somewhat mystically of the charms of a federal core of '*l'Europe-puissance*' being surrounded by an outer tier of '*l'Europe-espace*'. Lately, a more disillusioned Giscard has proposed the creation of a federation of nation states based loosely on the euro, run by a *Directoire* dominated by France and Germany. This set up, which he calls Europa, would have a secretariat sitting in Strasbourg and an occasional *congrès des peuples* composed of one-third MEPs and two-thirds MPs.[161] This core group would co-exist within the wider 'Brussels' EU.

The Glienicker Group of German economists has also suggested that a new treaty for the euro should be drafted within the over-arching EU framework.[162] Such a new treaty could be built on a reformed version of the enhanced cooperation provisions, relieved of the two current inhibitions that they are only to be deployed as a last resort and that they cannot involve the exclusive competences of the Union (which include monetary policy). Articles 136 and 138 TFEU, as well as a new version of Article 352, would be key clauses of the new arrangements – with Article 352 shed of its present constraints that it cannot be used either to harmonise national law or in the field of CFSP. The economists foresee a special chamber of MEPs from eurozone countries. The eminent EU jurist Jean-Claude Piris has elaborated similar ideas about the avant-garde, but goes further in differentiating the new from the old. He would have a parliamentary assembly made up of national MPs from the eurozone, a Committee of Ministers, a separate executive authority (not the Commission), and a separate judi-

161 Valéry Giscard d'Estaing, *Europa: La dernière chance de l'Europe*, 2014. Members of Europa would be the eurozone minus the Balts, Greeks, Slovaks and Slovenes but plus Poland, *le moment venu*.
162 *Towards a Euro Union*, 18 October 2013, http://www.glienickergruppe.eu/english.html

cial tribunal which would respect ECJ jurisprudence in the same manner as the EFTA Court.[163] The influence of Piris was evident, possibly, in the decision to call the bluff of the British by devising the fiscal compact treaty.

The reality is, nevertheless, that there is only one 'core group' which can act as a motor of integration for the wider Union, and that is the eurozone. In January 2015 Latvia becomes the nineteenth state to adopt the single currency. All others with the sole exception of the UK, which has a permanent opt-out for as long as it chooses, and not excluding Denmark and Sweden, are bound by treaty commitments to continue to try to join the euro despite the current adverse circumstances. It must be a political priority for the Juncker Commission to step up the pace of what can be called the Union's internal enlargement. Economic convergence is an imperative of monetary union, but it will only be solidified if accompanied by fiscal integration, which itself implies a greater ambition for political unity.

In the next chapter we will try to draw some conclusions about what all or some of its members might do to better define the chimerical political union. That is Europe's real agenda for change.

163 Jean-Claude Piris, *The Future of Europe: Towards a Two-Speed EU?*, 2012.

6. POLITICAL UNION

For some years the European Union has been tiptoeing around the edges of political union.[164] It will soon be time to take the plunge. So, by way of preparation, what needs to be done to transform what we have now into a fully-fledged political union? In the previous chapters we have looked at some of the problems and some of the options already proposed by those who support the notion of deeper integration, as well as by those who don't. We recommend positively the approaches adopted by Penelope and the Fundamental Law, and are sceptical about the sense of aiming for less. The option of 'less' has often been tried. The achievement of 'more' will not materialise by accident, but only by dint of a change of direction towards a federal government and a quickening of the pace of integration.

The government

If the European Union is poorly governed now, as many assert, it is because it lacks proper government. Successive treaties have enlarged the Union's competences, but they have not accorded it an executive with powers commensurate with its responsibilities and aspirations.

---

164 See, for example, Joschka Fischer, *From Confederation to Federation: Thoughts on the finality of European integration*, 2000.

Elements of executive authority exist at the EU level, but they are dispersed and abstruse. The result is that the EU disappoints; it cannot fulfil its evident ambitions to improve the welfare of its citizens at home or their security abroad. As a polity it seems to drift.

Central to the thesis of this small book is that, faithful to the tried and trusted 'Community method' of Monnet, executive powers need to be concentrated in a reformed European Commission. There will always be an important role in the Union for the function of intergovernmental diplomacy at summit level between the member states, but that function should be restricted in the main to constitutional matters, to decisions affecting the membership of the Union, to the making of top appointments and to matters of high strategy in the realm of security and defence policy, such as Ukraine: all these things are properly *Chefsache*. The leaders may turn themselves into firefighters during a financial storm, but to manage economic affairs in more mundane times the role of the European Council should give way to that of the European Commission. The present situation where the Union luxuriates in having two executives, with two presidents, is unsustainable. The relationship between José Manuel Barroso and Herman Van Rompuy indeed proved uneasy for the pair of them and mystifying to others. If they differed in their views and decisions, there was at once a political problem. If, on the other hand, they said the same thing in the same place at the same time, why on earth have the two of them? Is it credible that the President of the European Council, as the Lisbon treaty says, should represent the Union in foreign and security policy 'at his level', while the President of the European Commission represents the Union for everything else?[165] Which other world leader has to divide himself up between economic and security affairs?

The role of the European Council, therefore, should be radically redrawn. Instead of being charged with the job of defining the general political direction and priorities of the Union, it should be re-directed to running the Council of Ministers. The prohibition on it acting in a legislative capacity should be lifted: indeed, the leaders should be enabled to sit from time to time as the General Affairs Council and to pass laws therein. This reform would ground the heads of government more deeply in EU matters than they are at present – one of Monnet's objectives – as well as bringing steering and coherence to the affairs of the ordinary Council formations. The debilitating rotating presi-

165 Article 15(6) TEU.

dency of the ordinary Councils can be safely abolished: in its place, each formation of the Council should elect its own chair for a period of at least one year. In the interests of coherence in the system, the minister elected to chair the Eurogroup should also chair Ecofin. The permanent President of the European Council would in effect be chair of the upper house of the Union's legislature: as such he, with the President of the European Parliament, would take up the co-presidency of the constitutive Conventions. In its constitutional role, the European Council should gain the right, co-equal with the Parliament, to sack the Commission.

In exchange, however, the President of the European Commission should normally assume the job of ensuring the external representation of the Union at summit level, subject to the scrutiny of the European Council and European Parliament. As president-elect, he should be given the licence to pick the college of whatever size he chooses from shortlists of three candidates, including a man and a woman, offered up by the states. In deference to the Commission's enhanced political powers as the federal government, its quasi-judicial responsibilities in competition policy would be hived off to an autonomous anti-trust authority. In contradistinction, the EU's many agencies, with the exception of the anti-fraud office OLAF and the European Public Prosecutor's Office should be brought back within the Commission's central administration. This would save money and improve accountability.

As far as competences are concerned, when the Euratom treaty is finally wound up within the European Union, nuclear safety will become an exclusive competence. Elsewhere we need a more functional and less legalistic approach to what the EU can and must do well, and what may be better left to its states. The concept of federal union does not demand the conferral of a classical general competence on the Union whereby states can no longer act if the Union has itself acted. Yet it would seem to require a broader and more flexible definition of shared competence – perhaps, as the Fundamental Law of the Spinelli Group has it, as a sharing of a general competence between the EU and its states in a larger number of specified areas.[166] This more pragmatic approach implies a modification of the rule whereby the states can no longer legislate in an area of shared competence once the EU has filled

166 Article 19 FL (ex-Article 4 TFEU).

the legislative space.[167] The number of specific supplementary competences, where the EU is excluded from legislative action and is confined merely to assisting the states, would shrink accordingly. The general approach, as we have noted before, is to make the new constitutional treaty of the Union less prohibitive and more permissive than the present treaties so that the EU can act convincingly and decisively across a wider spectrum of public policy.

We would also wish to facilitate the use of enhanced cooperation by a core group of integration-minded states, based on the eurozone but open to all who meet the convergence criteria. Accordingly, the two qualifications of last resort and non-exclusive competences in the existing rules for enhanced cooperation should be abolished. The scope of the flexibility clause should be modified similarly, as the Spinelli Group proposes.

The Council of Ministers should cede most of its executive powers to the Commission. That the Council still fixes farm prices, for example, is an anachronism born of the early post-War days when feeding Europeans was still high politics: today, Europe is well fed and largely urbanized. As a democratic safeguard it would be prudent, in those executive areas which are transferred, to introduce a special 'call-back' procedure under which both the Council and Parliament have an equal, if limited, right to revoke the Commission's decisions before they enter into force. This right of revocation in the executive field would be additional to the system of delegated acts and implementing measures in the legislative field introduced by Lisbon.

In the hope of making those bodies more useful, it should also be the Commission and not the Council which is made responsible for the modalities of the Economic and Social Committee and the Committee of the Regions. For such subsidiary institutional matters, organic laws subject to higher thresholds in Council and Parliament are a sensible option. A liberalisation of the decision-making procedures on seats and languages should also be attempted in the interest, if nothing else, of cost savings. Small changes here and there to the rigid constraints of Lisbon would make a lot of difference to the potential reception of the new constitutional treaty in the eyes of the attentive citizen: for example, a widening of the remit of the European Citizens' Initiative to include general political (and not just narrow legal) propo-

---

167 Article 2(2) TFEU & Protocol No. 25.

sitions, or enlarging the powers of the Ombudsman so as to be able to act as *amicus curiae* at the Court of Justice. Who knows, even flying the flag and singing the 'Ode to Joy' might help.

We have discussed previously the alternative approaches advanced by Penelope and the Fundamental Law to the question of how to amend the treaty amendment procedure for the future. Nothing else will be more difficult to decide upon in a new Convention. As far as ratification is concerned, a lower and a higher threshold can be envisaged, respectively, for policy and constitutional amendments. An EU wide referendum should be catered for. The key thing, however, is that in a federal union ratification by all states should not be a requirement for treaty amendments to enter into force. Another category of membership short of full membership is an essential addition to the constitutional armoury for domestic and international purposes. Membership of the federal core cannot be compulsory and will not always be suitable. A binary choice between accession and secession seems crude. To craft an alternative form of affiliation to the EU for states outside the core is a rational response to Europe's wider geopolitical realities. The proposal in the Fundamental Law for a new form of associate membership deserves further exploration.

Economic and monetary union at last

In making adjustments to the arrangements for economic and monetary union as first prescribed by the Treaty of Maastricht, the main objective should be to allow for the formulation of a common economic policy of the EU to supplement and underpin the mere coordination of national economic policies. A *common* economic policy does not mean a *single* economic policy in which one size fits all, but instead a policy which takes account of geographical and demographic disparities, macro-economic imbalances between debtors and creditors, economic cycles, rates of growth and competitiveness, as well as structural issues like education, technology and levels of corruption. The Commission needs all the instruments appropriate to its assigned objectives, including the ability to make specific arrangements with state and regional authorities committed to growth enhancing supply reforms.[168] It also

168 These would be an improved version of the 'contractual agreements' proposed by Merkel at the European Council in December 2013 but rejected by others (mainly on the grounds, one assumes, that she is German).

needs to acquire a much enhanced capacity for economic analysis. A Commission so empowered would help the ECB in its cyclical role. A common policy combining monetary, fiscal and economic measures would add to the mission of price stability the goals of deepening the single market and raising productivity and employment. In practical terms, an optimal result of the shift away from a failure to coordinate national policies towards an agreed common policy would be that instead of Germany saving and France and Italy spending, the reverse might be the case.

This new-style economic policy will need to be driven by the Commission, with a powerful Treasury Minister representing the eurozone in international financial negotiations without the say-so of the Council. The Treasury Minister will also take the lead in the political dialogue with the ECB and in supervising and correcting national budgetary performance. The Commission's treasury will run lending and borrowing at the federal level and be responsible for managing the additional fiscal capacity of the eurozone in the interests of counter-cyclical macroeconomic policy. As noted previously, the famous 'no bail out' clause needs to be amended to allow the eurozone states to establish a system for the progressive, common pooling of a portion of sovereign debt, subject to strict conditionality.[169]

The normal EU budget would continue to support the cohesion and competitiveness of the single market, but it must be expanded to endow the Union with the financial resources it needs to match the scale of its political ambition. This means a larger budget and a healthy dose of fiscal federalism in order to lighten the burden on national finance ministries. Loosed from its current restrictions, the EU must be enabled to budget for a deficit under the same excessive debt and deficit procedures which already apply to its states. Critically, unanimity must be replaced by QMV for the decisions on the Union's revenue system of own resources and the multiannual financial framework. An organic law, with higher thresholds required in both Council and Parliament, would be appropriate here. The duration of the MFF should be set at five years to let more flexibility and democracy into budget making. In the event that there is no agreement on a new MFF, the previous framework should be carried forward, but adjusted for inflation. As far as the annual budget making procedure is concerned, a return

169 Revision of Article 125 TFEU.

to the pre-Lisbon formula would be appropriate whereby not only the Parliament but also the Council have to take political responsibility for the passage or rejection of the budget in the event that no conciliation between them proves possible. This will serve to make an eventual and realistic budget agreement more likely than not.

To maximise their political impact, the European Parliament should be consulted about and vote on macro-economic policy guidelines, and again before any necessary corrective recommendations are applied. Commission proposals under the excessive debt or deficit procedure must stand unless the Council opposes them by QMV without the participation of the errant state. Where the state does not accept the recommendations made to it, the Council could propose tougher measures, which might include penalties, on a proposal of the Commission. The national parliament of the state concerned should have the formal right to be heard by the EU institutions. The prohibition on the right of the Commission or a state to bring an action in the Court of Justice in the context of the excessive deficit procedure should be lifted. Lastly, states' direct GNI contributions to the EU budget should not be taken into account in assessing an excessive deficit.

The treaty should be adjusted to provide for the new functions of the European Central Bank in respect of the macro-prudential supervision of the entire financial sector, not just the banks. The creation of a single EU financial authority unifying the, at present separated, agencies should be catered for in the treaty revision. The Central Bank should become the Union's lender of last resort with a more broadly defined policy role backed up by a fully adequate capacity for analysis and supervision. In respect of the banking union, the ECB's new accountability to the Parliament should be codified in primary law along with other recent crisis innovations, including the normalisation of the European Stability Mechanism.

Modernising the common policies

The new Commission is in a strong position to propose to the Convention the systematic modernisation of the common polices of the Union, sector by sector. Three changes should command a high priority, however. First, in the light of the economic crisis, the EU needs to upgrade employment policy to become an integral criterion of a highly competitive social market economy. Second, in response to the ecological crisis, the fight against global warming should be added to the objectives of environment and energy policy. Third, faced with its immigration pressures, the Union should aim for integrated border management and true burden sharing, linked to both labour market and humanitarian policies.

More specifically, civic rights based on the Charter and germane to the concept of EU citizenship should be enlarged. The horizontal clauses that qualify the field of application and the scope of the Charter should be adjusted in order to let the Charter breathe, as is proper for a Bill of Rights in a federal polity. There should be a normalisation of the currently abnormal legislative procedures for anti-discrimination policies, for freedom of movement, for the right to vote and stand in municipal and European Parliamentary elections, and for consular protection. In order to redress an injustice whereby many Europeans living abroad are deprived of the right to vote either for their original national parliament or for the national parliament of the state in which they reside, it is important to extend, under certain residency conditions, the right of EU citizens living in states other than their own to vote for their local national parliament.

We would eliminate the prohibition on tax harmonisation within the internal market in order to simplify taxation for cross-border business and to facilitate the mobility of labour by introducing minimum terms and conditions for the treatment of taxation, mortgages, pensions and welfare benefits.[170] In order to further strengthen the social dimension of the single market, it should be made possible, at least for the eurozone, to harmonise national employment legislation and even to address matters of pay. In the area of labour law, reflecting the jurisprudence of the Court of Justice, it would seem necessary to confirm and clarify the right of the social partners to engage in collective labour agreements across the EU.

The Fundamental Law has presented some interesting ways to sharpen the treaty definitions of several of the current common policies. This includes the CAP and CFP, which should be disentangled from each other and given a new stress on food security, animal welfare and ecological sustainability. The Common Agricultural Policy is no longer abnormal, and should assume a more modest place alongside and in tandem with the other EU common policies that require an internal market regulated by a European Commission fully endowed with all the requisite instruments of policy management. Likewise, with the CFP, on fish quotas.

EU transport policy dates back to the Treaty of Rome, at a time

---

170 Revision of Article 114 TFEU.

when Europe's borders were almost closed, and is anomalous. Transport should today be treated like any other service industry under normal internal market rules. To the goals of the common transport policy a provision might be added to allow the EU to take charge of modernising cross-border transport systems according to high standards of technology and protection of the environment.

Consistent with the upgrading of environment policy, the treaty's energy chapter should also be revised to drop the absolute prohibition that EU policy must not affect a member state's unilateral right to determine its own choice of energy supply. Such a change implies a significant extension of the Union's competence in energy, without which it will be nigh impossible to build the Energy Union which Jean-Claude Juncker favours. Both the supply and demand side of a common EU energy policy should be structured to reflect the general interest of the Union as a whole, not least the combating of climate change, regardless of geographical and geological differences. The goal must be to build an interoperable energy grid for the whole Union in which supply is consistent, prices competitive and carbon emissions perpetually reduced.

Changes to the treaty in respect of justice and home affairs could speed the development of common policies for visas, asylum and both regular and irregular immigration. The quality of political union will be defined in part by how effective it is in managing the control of its external frontier. Greater emphasis could be placed on the principle of the mutual recognition of the different legal systems and traditions of the member states, and in legislating at the EU level for administrative cooperation between the national authorities. In cases of an emergency inflow of refugees, the Commission should be empowered to adopt provisional measures. As far as the integration of immigrant populations is concerned, and action against crime, the prohibition on the harmonisation of national law should be abolished. In matters of criminal justice and police, the 'emergency brakes' given by Lisbon to any one state should be dropped, and opt-outs phased out.

Streamlined international policies

European foreign policy needs to be radically rethought. Faced with growing insecurity and its continuing decline in global power politics, the EU must escape from its outdated and lazy clichés of 'strategic partnerships', 'neighbourhood policy' and 'comprehensive approach'. The change of leadership in the EU and at NATO coupled with the prospect of treaty change can combine to bring about a new division of labour between the EU institutions, its states and its close allies.[171]

A treaty change is needed to re-focus the European Council on setting the strategic orientation of the Union in international affairs, leaving to the Commission and Council the job of taking operational decisions, and to the High Representative and the Commission the role of initiating and coordinating policy. The High Representative must be allowed to take the lead in speaking for the Union in international fora, not least at the UN. The restriction on the authority of the European Court of Justice to adjudicate over operational aspects of common foreign, security and defence policy should be lifted.

The European External Action Service, on whose creation so much time and trouble has been expended since 2009, is dysfunctional. Unloved by both the Commission and the state governments, the EEAS suffers from internal rivalry and officious bureaucracy. The management of the EU's external relations puzzles third countries and weakens the European negotiating performance in international affairs. To end the turf wars and improve the coherence of all aspects of external policy, as well as the conjunction between internal and external security, the next Convention should concede that the EEAS experiment was of its time and has failed. To rebuild the toolbox, the External Action Service should be brought entirely within a revived Directorate-General of External Relations of the Commission. Jean-Claude Juncker's decision to invite the new High Representative, Federica Mogherini, back into the Berlaymont building from across the Rond-Point Schuman is a good start. National diplomats on secondment should continue to rotate in and out of the EU's reformed foreign ministry as a normal and natural part of their *formation professionnelle*. There will be cost savings.

Lisbon has bequeathed a highly convoluted decision-making procedure for CFSP. In the light of experience, it should be possible to admit that the Council will normally act by qualified majority vote. This does not preclude the fact that ministers of foreign affairs will normally prefer a consensual approach, but it would lighten the shadow cast by the threat of a unilateral national veto. Recourse to the European Council should be a last resort in cases of serious disagreement. The role of the European Parliament in CFSP could be much enhanced

171 See Nick Witney et al, *Rebooting EU Foreign Policy*, ECFR Policy Brief, October 2014.

by giving it the right of consent to decisions of the Council, subject to the observance of strict time-limits. In any case, MEPs should be informed and consulted over the conduct of foreign and security operations in addition to the 'main aspects and basic choices' of foreign policy as a whole. Rightly, Parliament also wants a strengthened role on the budgetary aspects of CFSP.

In security and defence policy, the EU battle-groups merit a specific legal base in the treaty. The role of the European Defence Agency would be strengthened by giving a more central role to the Commission and through the involvement of the European Parliament. Parliament should also have consultative powers in the establishment of a permanent military core group of the Union.

The scope of the commercial policy should be widened from foreign direct investment to include all investment, a change which would reduce the number of over-complicated 'mixed' EU and intergovernmental agreements. The Commission would take over from the Council the power to impose sanctions against third countries, subject to revocation by either the Council or Parliament. In overseas aid and development, EU states which wish to conduct their own supplementary international policies with third countries should be obliged to inform the Commission in advance. The purpose is to integrate more closely residual national development aid policies with the Union's common policy. This will be helped if the European Development Fund is incorporated into the general budget of the EU.

The arrangements for the EU's international agreements need a more radical overhaul. Several adjustments are needed to simplify and rationalise the procedures. The Commission should be able to prompt the Council to open an international negotiation, even in foreign and security policy matters; and the Commission must be the negotiator on behalf of the Union as a whole. Parliament's consent should be required both to authorise and to conclude all international treaties of the EU, including those in the field of CFSP. Decision-making procedures for international treaties must mirror those used for the Union's internal rules.

Constitutional interdependence

Treaty amendment of the type suggested here would establish beyond doubt the primacy of the European Commission as the government of the new polity, but it would be a government strictly held to account by the scrutiny of the bicameral legislature made up of the Council of Ministers and the European Parliament. Many interesting and desirable reforms have surfaced in the discussion in the previous chapters. It should be emphasised again that drafting a constitution builds the framework for efficient and democratic government: it should not anticipate or pre-empt the direction of future policy. The basics are fairly simple. The ordinary legislative procedure of co-decision between Council and Parliament will be the norm. Nothing would be admitted by the executive beyond the stretch of EU law; no law could be passed without the consent of both Houses; and no money could be spent that was not accounted for in the general budget of the EU. The European Council would play a larger part in the legislative activity of the Union, and would have important reserve powers of a strategic and constitutional nature. We would propose the drafting of a hierarchy of norms in the legal order of the Union, including an organic law for institutional matters.

The European Court of Justice will evolve naturally into the role of a federal supreme court. It should be admitted into basic constitutive processes, such as the verification of a breach of the Charter or consideration of a treaty amendment. The evolution of the ECJ in Luxembourg will accelerate once the Union accedes to the ECHR, allowing its judges to develop a superior body of jurisprudence in fundamental rights based on the Charter, all the time respecting the external supervision of the European Court of Human Rights in Strasbourg. The new treaty should make explicit the primacy of EU law and include, if possible, a new provision which codifies the principle of the direct effect of EU law. The reform of the ECJ, already underway, should be revisited. Greater continuity among judges and a higher degree of specialism – for instance in rights law, patents, financial services or data protection – would be desirable goals.

The constitutional role of the ECJ is destined to grow as the judiciaries of the member states take greater cognisance of their interdependent reliance on each other to faithfully and uniformly interpret EU law. A significant milestone was passed in February 2014 when the Bundesverfassungsgericht made its first ever preliminary reference to the ECJ, on the matter of whether the decision of the European Central Bank on Outright Monetary Transactions (OMT) is *ultra vires*. Other supreme courts, including the Spanish and Italian constitutional courts, the French Conseil d'Etat and the British House of Lords and Supreme Court make frequent applications to Luxembourg, but for Germany this sets a precedent. The Karlsruhe judges, as we have seen, have little compunction in opining about EU matters, so a greater degree of interaction is welcome. It may also encourage other national courts – for example, the Portuguese court, which has intervened to block parts of the EU's troika programme – to follow suit. Such a knitting together of the judiciaries would do much to foster the idea, important for the citizen, of a European area of freedom, security and justice. We have already commended, in this context, the idea in the Spinelli Group's Fundamental Law of a new 'reverse thrust' clause, whereby respect is due by the states to the constitutional identity of the European Union and not merely by the Union to the constitutional identity of its states. Illuminating the constitutional interdependence of the states will bring greater profile to the unique constitutional identity of the European Union.

Freeing up national parliaments

In these circumstances, one certainly needs to review the role of national parliaments in the Union architecture. It is abnormal in a federation (as opposed to a confederation) to have the parliaments of the member states interfere in the activity of the government or legislature of the federal polity. But because of the incomplete and unstable condition of the European Union, and because of domestic pressures within many EU states, national parliaments have become increasingly preoccupied by EU affairs. In the interests of building a decent parliamentary Europe, this engagement should not be at all discouraged. On the contrary.

Nevertheless, the subsidiarity early warning mechanism leaves much to be desired. Several national parliaments are frustrated that the 'yellow card' procedure has so seldom reached the required treaty threshold, and complain that in any case the limited focus on subsidiarity – at best a complex legal notion – is too narrow to provide for proper political scrutiny of the EU's draft legislation. Moreover, as we have seen, there is not evidently a large problem of disrespect by the European Commission for the principle of subsidiarity. While distracted on the false trail of subsidiarity, most national parliaments, for whatever reason, miss the opportunity to hold properly to account their own government ministers for their performance in the European Council and Council. Minor adjustments to the subsidiarity early warning mechanism could be made, but they would not in themselves produce significant improvements in the European dimension of the work of national MPs, and they might well further complicate the already fairly complex and lengthy legislative process at the European level.

That being the case, it would seem better to abolish the entire subsidiarity procedure, to liberate national parliaments from the straitjacket imposed by Protocol No. 2, and to encourage those parliaments to give freer expression of their political opinions in order to influence the EU institutions at any stage of the legislative process and across the whole spectrum of EU policy.[172] The EU has no need to patronise national parliaments: if they wish to organise their own conference in Strasbourg – an upgraded COSAC, without the involvement of the European Parliament – they should be allowed to do so. A revised Protocol No. 1 and the suppression of Protocol No. 2 could accommodate this step and serve to enhance the role of national parliaments in EU affairs.

Regional or 'sub-national' parliaments with legislative powers should also be encouraged to find their voice in EU matters. The current Committee of the Regions is not an adequate vehicle for these parliaments, and their presence alongside representatives of local government limits the usefulness of that body even for local authorities. As an increasing number of EU member states are federal or quasi-federal systems in their own right, parliamentary Europe must be construed to include rather than exclude regional parliamentary governments from privileged interaction with EU institutions.

Big versus small

There remains the thorny issue of the balance of power between larger and smaller member states as represented in the Parliament and Council. The new Convention should quickly re-visit the proposal on the seats tentatively advanced in the Parliament in 2011 known as 'Cam-Com'.[173] The CamCom method apportions seats in the Parliament according to an arithmetical formula that gives each state a base of five seats plus an allocation in proportion to the size of their population (subject to rounding upwards, and capping at the maximum). A divisor (d) adjusts the outcome to fit the overall size of the House (currently at 751 seats), where (P) is the population and (A) is the allocation function, rendered mathematically as:

$$T(d) = \sum_i [Ad(Pi)]$$

172 The early warning mechanism applies only to the non-exclusive competences.
173 For a full explanation see Geoffrey R. Grimmett, 'European Apportionment via the Cambridge Compromise' in Jean-François Laslier, Guest Editor, Special Issue, 'Around the Cambridge Compromise: Apportionment in Theory and Practice', *Mathematical Social Sciences*, vol. 63, no. 2, March 2012.

A variant of the formula would introduce the full CamCom in two stages so that no state loses more than two seats at the next elections in 2019.[174] The political benefit of CamCom is to eliminate the bartering process that has governed the distribution of seats in the Parliament to date: such increased transparency should elicit greater trust. Importantly, CamCom also respects the principle of equal voting power evenly distributed among the states, on which the Bundesverfassungsgericht has opined. Adjustments would be simply made during each five-year mandate of the Parliament to reflect demographic trends, population mobility, the number of member states of the Union, and the creation of transnational lists for a pan-European constituency.[175]

Even the comparatively straightforward decision – a 'pragmatic solution' – to award Croatia 11 seats in the 2014 Parliament, although consonant with the logic of CamCom, was only achieved by hard bargaining inside Parliament and between Parliament and Council.[176] So it is good news that the European Council decided at that stage to commit itself in principle to finding a durable arithmetical formula in good time before 2019.[177] The heads of government asked the Parliament to present its proposal in 2016.

The main practical effect of CamCom is to favour the larger and smaller states of the Union at the expense of the middle sized in line with the principle of degressive proportionality. So any Convention will need to re-open the question of voting weight in the Council in order to ensure that the overall balance of power in the Union legislature is equitable for all states and citizens. The Lisbon system to calculate basic QMV, introduced finally in November 2014, requires 55% of the states representing 65% of the population. This method gives the larger states a relative advantage over the Nice system where 255 votes were required (out of 345) representing 62% of the population. Although losing out on the second criterion of population size, small states benefit from the shift to the Lisbon rules because of the larger number of states (sixteen) required to reach the first threshold: medium-sized states do not benefit to the same extent.

174 See Annex Two.

175 For the full legal proposal, see Protocol No. 3 FL.

176 Report on the composition of the European Parliament with a view to the 2014 elections (2012/2309(INI)), (Gualtieri-Trzaskowski Report), A7-0041/2013.

177 European Council Decision 2013/312/EU, OJ L 181, 29-06-2013.

The question which the Convention needs to confront is whether votes in the Council should be allocated according to the square root of the population, which would accord voting power in inverse proportion to size.[178] The square root method, first advanced by Lionel Penrose in 1946, has increasing credibility in the academic literature, and a version named the Jagiellonian Compromise (JagCom) was proposed to the Giscard Convention by Poland.[179] Its adoption would correct the advantage in terms of voting clout accorded under the Lisbon scheme to the four largest states (Germany, France, UK and Italy), and benefit all the middling states (from Spain to Lithuania). The next Convention surely needs to establish a mathematical working group to consider the complementary merits of CamCom and JagCom. A fair outcome, one which improves the efficacy of decision making in the EU and adds to the system of federal checks and balances, would surely contribute to the growth of public trust in the governance of Europe's new polity.

In the last chapter we will conclude with a discussion of how and when the EU might best take forward this agenda for constitutional reform.

178 See Annex Three.
179 See Laslier et al, op cit; Wojciech Słomczyński & Karol Życzkowski, *Voting in the European Union: The square root system of Penrose and a critical point*, 2004; and Friedrich Pukelsheim, *Proportional Representation: Apportionment Methods and Their Applications*, 2014.

7. A CONVENTION AGAIN

The European Union has had more than its fair share of constitutional experiments in the last few years, some impressed upon it by *force majeure*, others invented and promoted in a more considered and systematic fashion. We should not let that rich experience go to waste. Nor should we fail to ensure that all the opportunities provided by the Treaty of Lisbon to strengthen the governance of the Union are exploited in parallel with constitutional reform. Here the change of the leadership team in late 2014 from Herman Van Rompuy, José Manuel Barroso and Catherine Ashton to Donald Tusk, Jean-Claude Juncker and Federica Mogherini (not forgetting Frans Timmermans) should provide fresh political will and impetus to the life of the institutions.

Both the Commission and the Council still have work to do to complete the full implementation of the Lisbon treaty with respect to inter-institutional relations, especially where co-decision is a novelty in the fields of agriculture, fisheries, trade, and justice and home affairs. The Council has issues to address about its own openness both in terms of its internal law making and in relation to the transparency of the lobbyists who crowd it. All institutions, not excluding the Parliament, should pay more attention to the quality of their assessment of the impact of draft law and amendments tabled to it. The European Parliament should address the problem of the random quality of its committee chairs and rapporteurs. A more meritocratic approach among MEPs, less hidebound to the D'Hondt formula for dealing out jobs and less held captive by national delegations, would raise the quality of law making, political scrutiny and media relations. National parliaments, meanwhile, would do well to stop treating European Union affairs as if they were a tiresome adjunct to foreign policy: much sharper scrutiny by MPs is needed in particular of the performance of their head of state or government in the European Council.

The top political priority is economic. If European integration cannot rise to the challenge of economic stagnation, democratic support for the European project is certain to be further and perhaps critically diminished. By not providing the Union with all the tools necessary to revive the economy, the limitations of Lisbon are already self-evident. Mario Draghi, the President of the European Central Bank, lets known his frustration that there cannot be a rebalancing of fiscal policy at the EU level without constitutional innovation and the creation of joint fiscal instruments. At the same time, however, the debate about 'genuine EMU' – banking, fiscal and political union – has stalled badly.

The evolving economic crisis coincides with the breakdown of the EU's relations with Russia, and a series of events which should strip Europeans of many delusions about stability and security in the post-Cold War period. How the EU and NATO respond to Russian irredentism and the phenomenon of failing states in the Middle East and North Africa may shape the future of the European Union in ways almost as important as its capacity to recover financial stability and economic growth. The new leadership of the EU institutions will be bound to take action to address the current widespread public sense of uncertainty and disillusion. A restoration of faith in European governance is urgent. As a starting point, all the institutions need time and space for a deeper reflection on the state of the Union. The basic question to address, in the light of what we know, is how a more united Europe might best be governed.

The rise and fall of the nation state

European history stands silent witness to attest to the importance of what contemporary Europeans are trying to do together in a peaceful and democratic way. The European Union is an ambitious historical experiment which deserves now to be accomplished, yet it is not a laboratory experiment but rather a pragmatic one, learning by doing out there in the real world.

In the seventy years since the end of the Second World War, Europe and Europeans have undergone great changes. For the founding fathers, building the first European Communities involved restoring the peacetime capabilities of the warring nation states. The state, restored to peace and liberty, was the building block of West European integration. The European Community symbolised restoration at the same time as it engineered the removal of national state barriers so as to bring stability and prosperity. Free trade and customs union between states led to anti-cartel policies and the formation of the single marketplace. Integration within the European Community solved the German problem for good as well as offering a new role for those countries which had already lost or were rapidly losing their colonies. After the fall of the Berlin Wall in 1989, the European Union continued in its role as the saviour of liberty, democracy and statehood to the benefit of the countries of the former Soviet bloc. Even Germany was restored as a fully unified state, though not in a way that Bismarck or Hitler would have recognised. The EU continues to work its magic, even if very slowly, in the Western Balkans. In terms of Europe's historical geopolitics, only the Russian and Turkish problems remain.

As their dependence on each other grew, the European nation states themselves were undergoing profound social and political transformation. Since the mid-1960s, the old certainties of race, church, class and privilege were contested by a younger, more liberal, multi-cultural and multi-ethnic Europe. Large-scale immigration from the former colonies from the 1950s onwards was joined shortly after the Millennium with a surge of mobility among European citizens taking full advantage of their right to exploit the free movement of people throughout the EU. Rapid globalisation saw the concentration of culture and finance in great cities, none larger than the metropolises of London to the West and Istanbul to the East. As far as the élites are concerned, European integration is one natural response of the region to the phenomenon of globalisation; the rise of the cosmopolitan European citizen, networked in social media, is another. The old order with its national, highly structured and centralised states has had to adapt to accommodate these trends: those for whom adaptation is difficult, above all the poorly educated, indigenous working class, are easily alienated. Nationalism has its constituency.

The transfer of national state sovereignty to the EU polity may be the logical expression of interdependence in the face of globalisation, but the loss of sovereignty has contributed to a lessening of political capability at home. Many of the most sensitive political issues – jobs, climate, health, energy, security – are of a scale that has transcended that even of the largest European nation states. The national political class has become less confident of being able to meet the expectations of the electorate. As Jean-Claude Juncker memorably remarked, 'We all know what to do, we just don't know how to get re-elected after we've done it'. The voter, as usual a step ahead of the political class, has noticed the pretentious nature of the claims of national political parties to do what they claim to be able to do at each and every election. Traditional electoral participation falls steadily away as the old states fail to deliver the goods. Meanwhile, at the European level, federal politics are taking their time to develop. Formal and rather good representative institutions – not least the European Parliament – have been created by the EU, but they are bereft of some essential democratic sinews, like media and political parties, which in any normal polity serve to connect the citizen with power. Inevitably there is popular resistance to a Brussels elite which is seemingly insensitive to the anxieties and aspirations of the electorate and can be clumsy and inadequate in explaining itself. As Jacques Delors said, 'You cannot fall in love with the single market'. So Europe today finds itself in a dangerous interregnum between the fading of national democracy and the rise of federal democracy. This half-way house is a risky place to stop.

The democratic crisis of the state in Europe is exacerbated by the rise of assertive cities and provinces. While the nation states struggle to respond to the centripetal imperative of the European Union, they are assailed by centrifugal pressures at home. National state constitutions are challenged by a resurgence of regional political forces, nowhere more powerfully than in Catalonia, Flanders and Scotland, but evident elsewhere too, as in Italy. The pressure for constitutional reform has been accentuated markedly by the financial crash and its social consequences. Emergency surgery by the EU may have saved its banking system, but the crisis seems now to have transferred from Europe's banks to its states. Whether the current state establishments in Greece, Italy or France can deal effectively with their sovereign debt crises is open to question. As they continue to fight growing public deficits, Spain and the UK experience constitutional turmoil. Even in Germany, where growth has stalled, the debate gathers pace about a revision of the settlement between Berlin and the Länder.

On top of this democratic ferment sits a European Union which, despite the installation of supranational institutions, is still mainly controlled by the governments of those troubled nation states. But uneasy lies the head that wears a crown. National politics is in a febrile state across Europe as the traditional ruling class tussles with the shifting paradigms of globalisation, European unity and neo-provincialism. The EU is an expedient that can usefully be blamed by politicians for all manner of wrongs. In particular, meetings of the European Council become a media circus at which mainly national-based journalists on day-trips to Brussels tend to play up only stories that show the EU failing chaotically to deal with its problems. For national governments and media, the part-time and barely accountable nature of the European Council is an ideal distraction from the daily grind of domestic politics. One can perfectly well see why member states prefer to cling to these intergovernmental, incremental ways of doing things, all the while paying lip-service to the Monnet method. But it is not a good way to govern the European Union. The financial crash and its aftermath have demonstrated well how the intergovernmental approach leads to centralisation around one German economic model of uber-competitiveness – alas, a model which does not work everywhere. As the EU ceases to deliver on its early promise of economic prosperity and a fair deal for all, so its own reputation sinks. The future of the Union will be in real doubt if it continues to rely for its economic governance on a cabal among member states. Even were the British to leave, a remaining confederal European Union would struggle hard in these interesting times to sustain the momentum of integration.

Our other model of full-time government is better – a federal democracy held accountable by, and responsible to, strong parliamentary forces at the European, national and regional levels. In a federal union the EU member states will not disappear: they will continue to be the constitutional basis on which the Union is founded, but the political dynamics will belong more to the EU citizen engaged in democratic life at the European as well as at the local, regional and national level. So we need not be wholly pessimistic. A sense of European Union citizenship is developing, not least among the 'Erasmus generation' (so called after the EU's popular student exchange scheme). New provincial polities latticed together, each with substantially devolved powers, are emerging to challenge the once exclusive authority of the nation state. These new forces, with English as lingua franca, can be harnessed to come to the aid of the European project.[180] It is not far-fetched to think of a future European Union as being more of a post-national constellation of autonomous city states and regions, rather than the collective of nation states we are used to today. Europe's new federalism would be recognisable to those who invented self-government in medieval Flanders, or indeed to Pierre-Joseph Proudhon, the advocate of subsidiarity in post-Jacobin France. Certainly the European Union, if it is to serve its citizens well, is required to be ever-inventive and adaptable to social and political change. In many ways it seems

180 See Philippe Van Parijs, *Linguistic Justice for Europe and for the World*, 2011.

already more attuned to the rhythm of the contemporary age than that of the old state system it has rescued from the ruins of war. Indeed, the sense that history is ineluctably on the side of integration is one reason why the EU's nationalist opponents are so infuriated by it.

The third Convention

We described earlier the European Union's constitutional progress, somewhat tortuous and protracted, which led from Nice and Laeken to Lisbon, via the Convention on the Future of Europe. We have examined the impact of all this on the present, crisis-ridden state of the Union. We have concluded that it is now time for the Union to take its next steps towards a constitutional settlement, but only in so far as those steps lead boldly in the federal direction. More pussy-footing will not do: indeed, more temporisation and dissembling may lead to the very break-up of the Union we are attempting to salvage and strengthen. Choosing the intergovernmental route may be easy, indeed lazy, but it will lead to an over-centralised technocratic Europe and provoke democratic resistance.

That the weight of current commentary is overwhelmingly anti-federal does not make it right. There will be many who, claiming 'treaty fatigue' and alleging the Union's limited capacity to integrate, will always do whatever they can to avoid a general revision of the EU treaties with a large agenda and ambitious goals.[181] Struck helpless by the myth of Pandora's Box, they are the people who have already lost faith in the European project and may have even lost hope – Pandora's last virtue – that European unification is worth it. Others will be certain to seek only a small treaty revision, taking refuge in tinkering at the edges, doing just enough to keep the bailiffs and the lawyers at bay. Those people will be of a conservative bent, naturally fearful of the emergence of post-national democracy as a vibrant force and sceptical that the time is yet right to give birth to a new sovereign polity of a cosmopolite Europe. Both of these two camps, the hopeless and the timid, preach about 'reform' of the EU without conviction or purpose. Such politicians expect the markets to take risks they are not

---

181 See, for example, Pierre de Boissieu et al, *Remaking Europe: Framework for a policy*, Synopia Report, September 2013, www.synopia.fr. A refreshing alternative, however, is Janis Emmanouilidis, Rapporteur, *Towards a New Pact for Europe*, 2nd Report, October 2014, www.newpactforeurope.eu.

prepared to take themselves. In doing so, they only bring comfort to the nationalists who would willingly put an end, if they could, to European integration.

Three alternative scenarios for the political reform of the European Union have surfaced in this book. The options are, put simply, to do nothing, to do little or to go federal. Our direction, inspired by history and driven by logic, is federalist. We insist that reform of the European Union must be structural because it is only a constitutive process which can realise the potential of the new polity in a legal and democratic way. Without a genuine constitutional approach no legitimate government of the Union will emerge. Fortunately, if a little by accident, the Union possesses a perfectly good and legitimate constitutive instrument in the Convention. Borrowed from Philadelphia in 1787, with a nod to the *Jeu de Paume* in 1789 and the anti-autocratic assemblies of 1848, the European Union has already braved two Conventions. Now is the time for the third.

Lisbon lays down how a Convention should be called and who should be convened to sit in it, but it does not determine the detail. There is, of course, precedent. The first Convention, which drew up the Charter of Fundamental Rights, was chaired by the ex-Federal President of Germany, Roman Herzog. The next, on the Constitutional Treaty, was chaired – and very much led – by the ex-President of the French Republic, Valéry Giscard d'Estaing. It is, frankly, unlikely that such a patriarchal figure as Giscard will be found again to preside over the new Convention. More likely is the emergence of a presidency team, or co-presidency, representing the two chambers of the EU legislature – in the present case, Donald Tusk and Martin Schulz. What is incontrovertible, however, is that for the Convention to succeed it will have to be driven by the work of the European Commission acting in two roles, that of Europe's think-tank and that of initiator of law. It falls in the first instance to the new college of Commissioners under Jean-Claude Juncker to lead the intellectual reflection on what should be done, and to prepare the political ground for a Convention to begin its work as soon as reasonably possible.

Juncker will have to act assertively to recruit the heads of government and MEPs to back the exercise of constitutional reform. According to Article 48(3) TEU, the European Council gets to trigger the process by a simple majority vote. It is critical that the European Parliament does not baulk at exercising its prerogative under the same article to insist on a Convention. The European Council cannot block the summoning of a Convention but it could make life very difficult if a steady majority of its members were not trustful of the exercise. Similarly, the European Parliament can insist on the calling of a Convention, but it is not able by itself to manage the treaty revision process in the absence of a sound partnership with the Commission.

During the preparatory phase a special responsibility falls on the government and parliament of the United Kingdom. David Cameron's call for a renegotiation of British terms of EU membership is perforce now one of the main driving forces behind the decision to have a third Convention. Philip Hammond, the new Foreign Secretary, told the House of Commons (17 October 2014) that he is proud to be 'lighting a fire under the EU' by legislating to hold an In/Out referendum in 2017. If the British renegotiation is to be remotely serious, however, threats will not work. Nor can the process be fast-tracked under the simplified treaty revision procedure. Removal of the mission to achieve 'ever closer union among the peoples of Europe' from Article 1 of the Treaty on European Union is no small thing: neither would be even its abbreviation to 'closer union', 'close union' or just 'union' – let alone its revision to 'federal union' as the Spinelli Group has proposed. However, beyond the usual reform rhetoric we have no real idea what the British Conservative Party is cooking up by way of renegotiation; nor do we know from the other parties in the Commons what their representatives will do once a Convention gets going. Writing some months before the event, it seems improbable that the British general election in May 2015 will succeed in clarifying Britain's European problem – which, for that matter, is also Europe's British problem. Whatever the outcome of that election, a divisive referendum on the future of UK membership within the next five years seems inevitable. Britain's partners badly need to know what kind of prospectus is more likely to keep the UK a member, and conversely what is likely to drive the British out. The Convention will have to reach a judgement on what price is worth paying to keep the British in; it would be very much amiss if it did not have a contingency plan for Brexit.

Careful preparation must also be undertaken by the European Parliament, as it was before the Convention on the Future of Europe under the guidance of the then chair of the Constitutional Affairs Committee, Giorgio Napolitano.[182] An important issue yet to be discussed is the

---

182 Fortunately, in the 2014 Parliament, the AFCO chair is Danuta Hübner, a former member of the European Commission and an active member of the Spinelli Group. Guy Verhofstadt has been appointed the Parliament's rapporteur for treaty change.

size of the Parliament's delegation to the Convention. In 2002 the delegation of MEPs numbered sixteen, one more than the then number of member states: this time one should expect a demand for more. Parliament's input to the Convention must concentrate on democracy and legitimacy, including those two elements where it has the formal right of initiative under Lisbon, namely seat apportionment and the uniform electoral procedure.[183]

The Commission, too, remembering Penelope, would do well to prepare itself to offer incisive political leadership to the Convention. In place of 'national where possible', the guiding motto of the new Juncker Commission should be 'fully federal where necessary'. One of the Commission's main challenges will be to make the Convention future oriented, addressing new problems like energy, climate and immigration which today out-stretch the nation state. Parliament and Commission working together must succeed in making the case for EU government.

A Convention will need enough time to find its own pace and create a dynamic. While there are good reasons not to rush a Convention into a premature conclusion, it is also true that the attention span of national leaders on constitutional matters is limited. Experience shows that the pressure of a timetable can work wonders in EU politics, notwithstanding the device of the stopped clock. On balance we would favour the introduction of a structured decision-making process for the close of the Convention involving the formal agreement of each of its four component parts. The lack of a Giscard will be telling: this time the members of the Convention will need to work out their own working methods conducive to reaching a democratic and intellectual consensus. To enhance the responsibility and the respectability of the Convention, its substantive recommendations should be allowed to stand unless overturned by a unanimous decision of the Intergovernmental Conference.

Timing is an important issue. Cameron threatens to hold his referendum in 2017, a seemingly arbitrary date which has no obvious connection with the reality of the European timetable. 2017 is also the year of the inevitably disruptive French and German elections. When to start and when to stop the Convention and subsequent IGC are questions more likely to be affected by how quickly Europe can recover from its prolonged economic slump. Economic confidence does won-

183 Respectively, Articles 14(2) TEU & 223(1) TFEU.

ders for public trust in constitutional reform. Other things being equal, it would seem desirable to aim to finish the constitutional business in 2019, possibly in connection with the next elections to the European Parliament.

Good public and media relations and decent consultation with civil society, business and NGOs will also make an important contribution to the building of a meaningful consensus. An introverted Convention would risk coming up with prescriptions which prove to be inexplicable or unjustifiable to the outside world.

Pre-eminent in the mind of the Convention will be the imperative to reach another constitutional moment for Europe, and not to botch it. The outcome must be a constitution for the European Union which will last for decades and provide a robust legal and democratic framework on the basis of which the political destiny of a more united Europe can be judiciously determined.

ANNEX ONE

A CHRONOLOGY OF EUROPEAN UNION TREATIES

Title	Signatories	Signature	Entry into force
Treaty establishing the European Coal and Steel Community (ECSC)	Belgium, France, Germany, Italy, Luxembourg, Netherlands ('The Six')	Paris 18 April 1951	25 July 1952 (expired 23 July 2002)
Treaty constituting the European Defence Community	The Six	Paris 27 May 1952	-
Treaty establishing the European Economic Community (EEC)	The Six	Rome 25 March 1957	1 January 1958
European Atomic Energy Community (EURATOM)	The Six	Rome 25 March 1957	1 January 1958
Treaty establishing a single European Council and Commission of the European Communities	The Six	Brussels 28 April 1965	1 July 1966
Treaty amending Certain Budgetary Provisions of the Treaties establishing the European Communities	The Six	Brussels 22 April 1970	1 January 1971
Act concerning the Accession to the European Communities of the Kingdom of Denmark, Ireland and the United Kingdom of Great Britain and Northern Ireland	The Six + Denmark, Ireland, Norway, United Kingdom	Brussels 22 January 1972	1 January 1973 (minus Norway)
Treaty amending Certain Provisions of the Protocol on the Statute of the European Investment Bank	The Nine	Brussels 10 July 1975	6 April 1978
Treaty amending Certain Financial Provisions of the Treaty establishing the European Communities	The Nine	Brussels 22 July 1975	1 June 1977
Act concerning the election of the representatives of the Assembly by direct universal suffrage	The Nine	Brussels 20 September 1976	1979

continued...

Title	Signatories	Signature	Entry into force
Act concerning the Accession to the European Communities of the Hellenic Republic	The Nine + Greece	Athens 28 May 1979	1 January 1981
Treaty amending, with regard to Greenland, the Treaties establishing the European Communities	The Ten + Denmark + Government of Greenland	Brussels 13 March 1984	1 February 1985
Act concerning the Accession to the European Communities of the Kingdom of Spain and the Portuguese Republic	The Ten + Portugal, Spain	Lisbon/ Madrid 12 June 1985	1 January 1986
Agreement between the Governments of the States of the Benelux Economic Union, the Federal Republic of Germany and the French Republic on the gradual abolition of checks at their common borders	Belgium, France, Germany, Luxembourg, Netherlands	Schengen 14 June 1985	1 January 1986
Single European Act	The Twelve	Luxembourg 17 February 1986 The Hague 28 February 1986	1 July 1987
Treaty on European Union (TEU)	The Twelve	Maastricht 7 February 1992	1 November 1993
Act concerning the Accession to the European Union of the Republic of Austria, the Republic of Finland and the Kingdom of Sweden	The Twelve + Austria, Finland, Sweden	Corfu 24 June 1994	1 January 1995
Treaty of Amsterdam amending the Treaty on European Union, the Treaties establishing the European Communities	The Fifteen	Amsterdam 2 October 1997	1 May 1999
Treaty of Nice amending the Treaty on European Union, the Treaties establishing the European Communities	The Fifteen	Nice 26 February 2001	1 January 2003

continued...

continued table

Title	Signatories	Signature	Entry into force
Act concerning the conditions of accession of the Czech Republic, the Republic of Estonia, the Republic of Cyprus, the Republic of Latvia, the Republic of Lithuania, the Republic of Hungary, the Republic of Malta, the Republic of Poland, the Republic of Slovenia and the Slovak Republic and the adjustments to the Treaties on which the European Union is founded	The Fifteen + Cyprus, Czech Republic, Estonia, Hungary, Latvia, Lithuania, Malta, Poland, Slovakia, Slovenia	Athens 16 April 2003	1 May 2004
Treaty establishing a Constitution for Europe	The Twenty Five	Rome 29 October 2004	-
Act concerning the conditions of accession of the Republic of Bulgaria and Romania	The Twenty Five + Bulgaria, Romania	Luxembourg 25 April 2005	1 January 2007
Convention between the Kingdom of Belgium, the Federal Republic of Germany, the Kingdom of Spain, the French Republic, the Grand Duchy of Luxembourg, the Kingdom of the Netherlands and the Republic of Austria on the stepping up of cross-border cooperation, particularly in combating terrorism, cross-border crime and illegal migration	Austria, Belgium, France, Germany, Luxembourg, Netherlands, Spain	Prüm 27 May 2005	1 November 2006
The Treaty of Lisbon amending the Treaty on European Union and the Treaty establishing the European Community	The Twenty Seven	Lisbon 13 December 2007	1 December 2009
Treaty establishing the European Stability Mechanism	The Seventeen States of the eurozone	Brussels 11 July 2011, 2 February 2012	27 September 2012
Act concerning the conditions of accession of the Republic of Croatia	The Twenty Seven + Croatia	Brussels 12 December 2011	1 July 2013
The Treaty on Stability, Coordination and Governance in the Economic and Monetary Union	The Twenty Seven minus the Czech Republic, United Kingdom	Brussels 2 March 2012	1 January 2013

ANNEX TWO

SEAT APPORTIONMENT IN THE EUROPEAN PARLIAMENT

Member State	Population (2014)	2014 Current MEPs	2019 CamCom phase one	2024 CamCom final
Germany	80780000	96	96	96
France	65856609	74	82	83
UK	64308261	73	80	82
Italy	60782668	73	76	77
Spain	46507760	54	60	61
Poland	38495659	51	50	51
Romania	19942642	32	30	29
Netherlands	16829289	26	25	25
Belgium	11203992	21	19	19
Greece	10992589	21	19	19
Czech Republic	10512419	21	19	18
Portugal	10427301	21	19	18
Hungary	9879000	21	19	17
Sweden	9644864	20	18	17
Austria	8507786	18	16	16
Bulgaria	7245677	17	15	14
Denmark	5627235	13	12	12
Finland	5451270	13	12	12
Slovakia	5415949	13	12	12
Ireland	4604029	11	11	11
Croatia	4246700	11	10	11
Lithuania	2943472	11	9	9
Slovenia	2061085	8	8	8
Latvia	2001468	8	8	8
Estonia	1315819	6	7	7
Cyprus	858000	6	7	7
Luxembourg	549680	6	6	6
Malta	425384	6	6	6
Total	507416607	751	751	751

ANNEX THREE
SQUARE ROOT VOTING IN THE COUNCIL

Member State	Population (2014)	Square Root value
Germany	80780000	8988
France	65856609	8115
United Kingdom	64308261	8019
Italy	60782668	7796
Spain	46507760	6820
Poland	38495659	6204
Romania	19942642	4466
Netherlands	16829289	4102
Belgium	11203992	3347
Greece	10992589	3316
Czech Republic	10512419	3242
Portugal	10427301	3229
Hungary	9879000	3143
Sweden	9644864	3106
Austria	8507786	2917
Bulgaria	7245677	2692
Denmark	5627235	2372
Finland	5451270	2335
Slovakia	5415949	2327
Ireland	4604029	2146
Croatia	4246700	2061
Lithuania	2943472	1716
Slovenia	2061085	1436
Latvia	2001468	1415
Estonia	1315819	1147
Cyprus	858000	926
Luxembourg	549680	741
Malta	425384	652
Total	**507416607**	**98776**

JagCom proposes a QMV formula equating to half the total population plus half the total weights, so that the quota is 60651.

A selection of other books from John Harper Publishing ...

Driving the EU Forward – Straight Talks with Maroš Šefčovič

In this short and accessible book from summer 2014, European Commission Vice-President Maroš Šefčovič argues that the EU must continue to move towards a more political union. His emphasis is on the practical steps that can and should be taken to improve people's lives and reconnect the EU with its citizens. And he is unapologetic in arguing for the continuing pivotal importance of the Commission to the European project.

Europe's Parliament: People, Places, Politics

Stephen Clark and Julian Priestley

An entertaining and richly informative insiders' view of what the European Parliament is really like, written by its former (1997-2007) Secretary General and current Director for Relations with Citizens. It brings to life the environment and atmosphere of Brussels, Strasbourg and Luxembourg; the MEPs and the staff; the internal politics; the personalities; and how the work is actually done. Illustrated throughout with more than 350 photographs.

The European Commission: A Practical Guide

Manuel Szapiro

This book is designed to be a practical guide to what the European Commission is, relevant to all who work for or with the Commission or have dealings with it. It explains the role of the College and the President, and how the administration is organised – the jobs people do, how they are recruited and the rules under which they operate. The book looks systematically at the Commission's powers, procedures and practices, and shows how it works with the other EU institutions and the wider world.

Influencing the Preparation of EU Legislation: A Practical Guide to Working with Impact Assessments

Erik Akse

This is a working tool for anyone with an interest in shaping EU legislation, including business organisations, regional and national governments, NGOs, citizen groups, law firms and public affairs professionals. It provides a detailed step-by-step guide to why, when and how the European Commission carries out Impact Assessments for proposed legislation – and how stakeholders can most effectively work with the Commission to ensure their issues and evidence are taken into account.

Building a Liberal Europe: The ALDE Project

Graham Watson

Graham Watson, who led the Liberal group in the European Parliament from 2002 to 2009, describes how it for the first time became a significant 'third force'. Politics and personalities combine to make this a fascinating and insightful insider's historical account which will be of interest to all who follow EU affairs and liberal politics.

For full details of all these books, as well as announcements of other forthcoming titles, please visit *www.johnharperpublishing.co.uk*